Conflicting Concepts of Holiness

CONFLICTING CONCEPTS OF HOLINESS

by

W. T. Purkiser

BEACON HILL PRESS OF KANSAS CITY
Kansas City, Missouri

First Printing, 1953
Revised Edition, 1972

Printed in the
United States of America

ISBN: 083-410-2781

10   9   8

Contents

Preface

No theme as important to Christian life as scriptural holiness should long go unexamined or can long go unchallenged. Our purpose in these pages is to consider some of the current issues relating to this aspect of the faith "once delivered unto the saints."

As here used, an issue is a point of challenge, of debate or contest. One cannot preach or teach any doctrine successfully without being conscious of the issues raised in the minds of those with whom he labors. Holiness literature is full of strong defense of this truth against issues of the past. While error has a sort of perennial quality about it—recurring in cycles generation after generation—it is always important to relate one's central doctrine to whatever turn the issues of the day may take.

Our particular concern here is with the issues presented to us in the context of modern evangelical Christianity. That is, we do not propose to discuss the Wesleyan view of full salvation against the background of what is commonly called liberalism, or against any view of the Christian faith that discounts the historic belief in the full inspiration and final authority of the Scriptures. I shall assume the essential truth and value of the traditional evangelical position that the Bible is the prime Source of all doctrinal truth and practical duty, and that the Book means just what it says when interpreted, as it always must be, in context.

The demand for cooperation among evangelical Christians in a "post-Christian" era points to the need for clear definition of issues. Christian unity cannot be gained by "levelling down" to the lowest common denominator of faith.

This means an obligation to relate what is distinctive in "holiness" faith to the issues presented by the larger associations that we cannot and should not try to avoid. We must be ready always to give strong reasons for the special facet of the hope we cherish.

That the present writer should be able to isolate and discuss all the issues is, of course, to expect too much in too brief a space. That he shall even name the most important issues must depend upon the extent to which his experience and contacts in evangelical circles are typical. He can hope to escape the criticism that this treatment is incomplete and unrepresentative only by pointing out that this purports to be a discussion of only *some* contemporary issues. There are others now; there will be more later. These are but representative of those which seem to come closest to the heart of the Wesleyan doctrine of entire sanctification.

One further point is important. Sharp issue will be taken here with some popular religious views. In no case should objections to a system of theology be taken as an attack on the Christian experience or character of those who hold that theology. A man's character may be much better than his creed—just as, conversely, it may not be as good. Some of the views considered here are held by Christian brothers and sisters in whose personal integrity and effectiveness of Christian service the writer has utmost confidence. We are often much closer in heart and experience than we are in the interpretation of experience.

This is not to say that one creed is as good as another, and that it really doesn't make any difference what one believes as long as he lives right. The usual outcome of wrong teachings is a misdirected life.

We propose to consider five major issues related to Christian holiness:

1. *Is holiness imputed or imparted?* Is the holiness of the saints a legal reckoning in the mind of God, or is it an aspect of personal moral character? We deal with this issue under the theme "Sanctification and Cleansing."

2. *Is holiness progressive or instantaneous?* Is it the ever-increasing counteraction of the carnal nature, or the momentary crucifixion of sin within? This is the subject of the second chapter, "Process and Crisis in Sanctification."

3. *What is the nature of actual sin in human life?* Is it deviation from an objective and perfect standard of righteousness, or willful transgression of a recognized law of God? The subject here is "Christian Perfection and Sin."

4. *What is the evidence or sign of the indwelling presence of the Holy Spirit?* Is there an outward manifestation, a gift of the Spirit, which certifies the reality of the baptism with the Spirit? This matter is discussed under "Sanctification and Signs."

5. *What is the basis of Christian security?* Is it an initial momentary act of faith, forever assuring the soul of final salvation; or is it entrance into "this grace wherein we stand, and rejoice in hope of the glory of God" (Rom. 5:2)? Here our theme is "Sanctification and Security."

Acknowledgments

The author gratefully acknowledges permission to use copyrighted material by Ralph M. Riggs, quotations from *The Spirit Himself*, published by the Gospel Publishing House of Springfield, Mo.; J. H. Strombeck, quotations from *Shall Never Perish*, published by the Strombeck Agency, Moline, Ill.; John R. Rice, a quotation from the booklet *Can a Saved Person Ever Be Lost?*; the magazine *King's Business*, a quotation from an article by Douglas C. Hartley on "The Security of the Believer"; the Loiseaux Brothers, Inc., a quotation from their book *The Epistles of John*, written by August Van Ryn; and the administration of the Dallas Seminary Press, quotations from *Systematic Theology*, by Lewis Sperry Chafer, Volumes III and VI.

Chapter 1

SANCTIFICATION AND CLEANSING

The heart of the Wesleyan doctrine of Christian holiness is the claim that God can and does actually, in this life, through the gracious gift of His Spirit, render the entirely consecrated believer "holy in all manner of conversation" by reason of being completely cleansed from inherited sin.

No teaching which denies such a cleansing can properly be called holiness in the sense in which we use the term. The essential point of the doctrine of entire sanctification is this fact of heart purity as an actual purging of the soul.

POSITIONAL HOLINESS

One of the major challenges to which this faith is subjected is from those who assert that no such cleansing is possible, and that the holiness of the New Testament is a positional holiness wherein the believer, who is in Christ, is said to be accounted holy while actually impure.

If I understand their meaning correctly, this is the view espoused by Dr. C. I. Scofield and the scholars who collaborated with him in the preparation of the Scofield Bible. It is the position, by and large, of the Bible institutes which have grown from the monumental work of Dwight L.

Moody, and of other outstanding institutions. Its contemporary vogue stems from the influence of the Plymouth Brethren in nineteenth-century England, and the Keswick Conference in this century. I mean no injustice to the varied facets of thought displayed by these different groups in thus lumping them together. They seem, however, to be agreed on the point of positional sanctification—or what is sometimes called the "holy in Christ" theory.

A typical summary of this is the statement of the Scofield Bible or Testament in the helps on Rev. 22:11. Here we are told that sanctification, when used of persons, has a threefold meaning. First, *in position*, believers are said to be eternally set apart for God by redemption, and "positionally" are saints and holy from the moment of believing. Scripture references for this statement are Phil. 1:1 and Heb. 3:1. Second, *experientially*, it is claimed that the believer is being sanctified by the Holy Spirit through the Scriptures. Third, *in consummation*, the believer's complete sanctification is said to await the return of the Lord.

It is the first meaning stated that concerns us here. There is said to be a holiness which is positional, but not experiential. All redeemed souls, we are told, are "saints" and "holy" even though they are still being "sanctified" by the work of the Holy Spirit through the Scriptures and will never be completely sanctified until Christ comes again. The last two claims—that sanctification is progressive in nature and completed only at death or the rapture—will be considered in the next chapter. The doctrine of positional holiness is the point in question for the moment.

If "positional" sanctification in the foregoing statement could be understood as "potential," I should have little argument. The facts are, however, it is not so understood by its authors. There is much underlying this statement which does not appear on the surface. The foundation of this entire school of thought is laid on at least five interrelated theses.

1. The Christian is said to possess two natures throughout his whole earthly Christian life—the seed of God, and the mind of the flesh or the carnal nature. These two natures are said to coexist in such fashion that the believer's actual conduct may be now under one, now under the other, without in any way affecting his standing with God.

2. Since the believer is in Christ and Christ is holy, the believer is holy in Christ, but not necessarily holy in character or conduct. That is, not only is the righteousness of Christ—His perfect obedience to God's law—imputed in justification to cover the believer's confessed sins, but the holiness of Christ—His conformity of nature to the character of God—is likewise supposed to be imputed to the believer. God is alleged to look at the believer through Christ, and to see him as holy even as Christ is holy, although in point of fact he may at that very moment be full of carnality and sin.

3. The believer's sin nature can never be destroyed in this life, thus leaving him under the partial, and sometimes the full, dominion of the mind of the flesh. However, the sins which result from this sinful nature are not, in the case of the believer, supposed to be subject to condemnation at the judgment bar of God. These are, allegedly, dealt with at the judgment seat of Christ in the dispensation of rewards.

4. The justification or forgiveness granted the believer when he first accepts Christ is a permanent justification and encompasses all the future sins he may commit, as well as all his past sins. Faith only is the ground for justification. Repentance, if mentioned at all, is the transient sorrow of the sinning Christian when he realizes he has lost fellowship or broken communion with God.

5. It follows from the foregoing that the believer's standing in Christ is eternal and unchangeable, no matter how fluctuating his moral state may be. This, now known as

the doctrine of eternal security, is basically the claim that any individual who is once saved can never be finally lost, regardless of his faith or lack of faith, his sinfulness or righteousness of life.

Points one and two concern us in this chapter. Points three and four will be considered in Chapter 3. The final point will be the subject of Chapter 5.

The Doctrine of the "Two Natures"

Let us turn then to these twin doctrines of the *two natures* and *imputed holiness*—the theory that while yet possessing the carnal nature we are "holy in Christ."

We shall deal only briefly with the doctrine of the two natures, inasmuch as the theory of positional holiness is more directly related to our overall theme. As usually presented, it is the belief that the seed of God implanted in the believer's heart at conversion is essentially another nature, incapable of sin, and tending to righteousness. Coexisting with this new nature is the old man, the carnal self, which is said to be indestructible, an essential part of our human mortality. Proof texts ordinarily given are John 3:6, *That which is born of the flesh; and that which is born of the Spirit is spirit;* and Gal. 5:17, *For the flesh lusteth against the Spirit, and the Spirit against the flesh: and these are contrary the one to the other: so that ye cannot do the things that ye would.*

If this were but an awkward way of describing the struggles of an unsanctified Christian with the tendencies of a carnal heart, one could have little objection to it. But it is much more than that. It is represented as the norm, the standard for Christian life—than which one can expect no more. It is contended that these two natures are so far independent of each other as each to be relatively unaffected by the actions of the other. Thus, the believer may act under the influence of the mind of the Spirit without thereby improving the mind of the flesh. Conversely—and here is the payoff—the believer may sin under the influence of the fleshly nature without the spiritual nature being essentially affected thereby.

Two observations should be made. First, it is psychological foolishness to represent human nature as so compartmentalized that one part of it may act without altering or affecting all the rest. Apart from abnormally split personalities, the human psyche is a dynamic unity, responding to diverse motivations as a total self, and modified continuously by every response. The two-nature view is in fact a sort of spiritual schizophrenia, a kind of religious Dr. Jekyll and Mr. Hyde.

Second, this theory is a virtual denial of the scriptural doctrine of the new birth. Nowhere does the Bible represent the new birth as the injection of a divine nature into an otherwise unmodified human nature. It is the human being who is born from above, not an abstract spiritual entity added to the soul. II Cor. 5:17 provides a healthy antidote for this error: *Therefore if any man be in Christ, he is a new creature: old things are passed away; behold, all things are become new.*

THE NATURE OF SCRIPTURAL HOLINESS

What, now, about the view that the holiness of the believer is "in Christ," not inherent in himself? Lewis Sperry Chafer, for instance, in Vol. VI of his *Systematic Theology* says, "*Positionally*, the 'old man' has been put off forever. *Experimentally* the 'old man' remains as an active force in the life which can be controlled only by the power of God."[1] If this is true, the Wesleyan doctrine of entire sanctification is not only false, but dangerous. It is therefore of utmost importance that we understand and clarify this issue.

One is, first of all, impressed by the almost complete lack of direct scriptural citation in support of this view. It appears motivated by a desire to eat the cake and have it too—to fulfill the requirement for holiness stated in the Word, "without which no man shall see the Lord," and to have license for the continued indwelling of sin. Holiness we must have, but if Christ is our Holiness as He is our Justification, then the believer may be holy positionally and carnal experientially.

Does the fact that the believer is "in Christ" warrant the conclusion that the believer is therefore positionally holy, however sinful he may be actually, both by nature and by deed? This we cannot see. The phrase "in Christ" is Paul's great designation of the true Christian. To be in Christ is to be so related to Him as to participate in the salvation He has made possible. It cannot be taken to mean that God fools himself into accounting a carnal heart holy because He sees that heart through the holiness of His Son.

The basic consideration here is that holiness is a quality of character and cannot be transferred. Christ is holy in himself, and if the Christian is holy at all he is holy by reason of having become actually a partaker of the divine nature.[2] This is, of course, Christ's work in the heart. But it is actual, and not merely logical. That Abraham believed God, and that it was accounted to him for righteousness, does not mean that faith is a substitute for righteousness. It means that faith is the condition whereby the heart is made righteous by a divine act.

The Bible does not lack for specific declarations of the actual holiness of an entirely sanctified heart. It presents such a state as the ideal and obligation of every believer. For example, I Pet. 1:15-16: *But as he which hath called you is holy, so be ye holy in all manner of conversation; because it is written, Be ye holy; for I am holy.* The holiness here commanded is not of a different sort, a *positional* holiness. It is qualitatively identical with the holiness of God. *"As he . . . is holy, so be ye holy."* Note the words "as" and "so."

I John 3:3, 7 adds its testimony at this point: *And every man that hath this hope in him purifieth himself, even as he is pure. Little children, let no man deceive you: he that doeth righteousness is righteous, even as he is righteous.* The purity here commanded is not different from that of Christ; and the believer's righteousness, rather than being imputed, is here said to be in exact correspondence to the righteousness of Christ.

Consider I John 4:17: *Herein is our love made perfect, that we may have boldness in the day of judgment: because as he is, so are we in this world.* Note again the words "as" and "so."

Look at Luke 1:73-75: *The oath which he sware to our father Abraham, that he would grant unto us, that we being delivered out of the hand of our enemies might serve him without fear, in holiness and righteousness before him, all the days of our life.* Here holiness and righteousness are portrayed as a quality of character in which we may serve God throughout this life.

HOLINESS AS ACTUAL CLEANSING

We go now directly to the New Testament for a synthesis of its teaching regarding actual cleansing—the complete purging of the heart from all inherited depravity. We shall consider briefly 10 references, taking them simply in the order of their appearance.

Matt. 3:11-12: *I indeed baptize you with water unto repentance; but he that cometh after me is mightier than I, whose shoes I am not worthy to bear: he shall baptize you with the Holy Ghost, and with fire: whose fan is in his hand, and he will throughly purge his floor, and gather his wheat into the garner; but he will burn up the chaff with unquenchable fire.*

Here we observe that the baptism with the Spirit as fire follows the baptism with water unto repentance. These cannot be concurrent without a hopeless mixture of figures. But the important point is that the purpose of Christ's baptism is the thorough purging of His "floor," gathering the wheat of sanctified human nature into the garner, and destroying the chaff of the carnal nature with the unquenchable fire of the Holy Ghost. This interpretation of the wheat and the chaff is not the only possible one, but it is the most natural one in the total context. The baptism with the Spirit and the purging of the floor are simultaneous—they go together.

Matt. 5:8: *Blessed are the pure in heart: for they shall see God.* Is it conceivable that our Lord should have pronounced such a blessing upon a class of persons which did not exist, and which could never exist on this earth in this dispensation? The rest of the Beatitudes admittedly concern qualities of character or conditions of life which are found in the Church throughout all ages—the poor in spirit, the meek, the peacemakers, the hungry and thirsty after righteousness, the persecuted. Why then should the pure in heart be placed in a different group, as referring to a class without members? It is much more true to the Scriptures to recognize that there are those whose hearts are pure, who enjoy the blessedness of seeing God.

Acts 15:8-9: *And God, which knoweth the hearts, bare them witness, giving them the Holy Ghost, even as he did unto us, and put no difference between us and them, purifying their hearts by faith.*

In these words, the Apostle Peter makes a direct identification of the baptism with the Holy Spirit and the purifying of the believer's heart by faith. After 15 years, the aspect of Pentecost which remained most significant to Peter was not the noise of a mighty rushing wind; not the cloven tongues of fire; not even the gift of other languages. It was the purifying of the heart in response to appropriating faith, upon receiving the fullness of the Spirit, whom the world cannot receive (John 14:17).

Rom. 6:6-7: *Knowing this, that our old man is crucified with him, that the body of sin might be destroyed, that henceforth we should not serve sin. For he that is dead is freed from sin.*

Many outside the holiness movement resent the term "eradicate" in reference to sin in the heart. We are not disposed to contend for a term which is extra-biblical, however useful it might be. We are willing to use scriptural terms. If our friends cannot admit eradication, why not just substitute "crucifixion" and "destruction" as God's method of dealing with "the old man"? Crucifixion was widely used in Bible times as a method of capital punishment. It always resulted in death. Never could this be construed to mean the suppression or counteraction of that which still lives on as an active force in the heart.

Likewise, to destroy certainly means—if not annihilation—at the very least the doing away with the body of sin. The whole tenor of this sixth chapter of Romans is that what Christ wrought for us on the Cross can and must be wrought in us by the Spirit of God.

Rom. 8:2: *For the law of the Spirit of life in Christ Jesus hath made me free from the law of sin and death.* This is in striking contrast to the seventh chapter of Romans, the classic passage for those who deny actual deliverance from carnality in this life. Paul had said there, "I am carnal, sold under sin. . . . when I would do good, evil is present with me. . . . it is no more I . . . but sin that dwelleth in me. . . . O wretched man that I am! who shall deliver me from the body of this death?" (Rom. 7:14, 21, 20, 24)

This, it is claimed, is the norm of Paul's religious experience. This represents the best possible attainment in grace. This shows that sin is inherent to the finite human, and cannot be avoided.

Does Romans 7 represent Paul's high-water mark in grace? Is this his description of a normal Christian experience, even that of a babe in Christ? The answer is an emphatic "No!" We have heard some rather sorry confessions of failure made by God's children, but never have we heard a genuinely born-again believer get up and testify, "O wretched man that I am!"

Paul is here vividly contrasting his old life as an awakened sinner striving in his own might to keep the law of God, with the deliverance he found in the regenerating and sanctifying grace of the Lord Jesus Christ. In the old life, he found in his heart a law that countered the ideal of his awakened conscience. He was, as he said, captive to the law of sin indwelling in his members, the body of death which made him wretched.

Then, using the same terminology, he describes the deliverance wrought in him by the Spirit of Christ. *The law of the Spirit of life in Christ Jesus hath made me free from the law of sin and death.* Here, as clearly as language can express it, is the claim of the Apostle Paul to freedom from the nature of sin and the body of death with which he had struggled so long in vain. Little wonder he shouts, *Thanks be to God through Jesus Christ our Lord* (see Rom. 7:25).

II Cor. 7:1: *Having therefore these promises, dearly beloved, let us cleanse ourselves from all filthiness of the flesh and spirit, perfecting holiness in the fear of God.*

Here is a total cleansing for those who have, by reason of sonship to God, *exceeding great and precious promises.* Lest Paul be charged with advocating sanctification by human effort, let it be said that we cleanse ourselves in the same way Peter said we should save ourselves from this perverse generation (Acts 2:40). In each case, it is by bringing ourselves into right relation to the saving and cleansing virtue of the blood of Christ. The point is, total cleansing "from all filthiness of flesh *and* spirit" is both necessary and possible as the basis for perfecting holiness in the fear of God.

Eph. 4:20-24: *But ye have not so learned Christ; if so be that ye have heard him, and have been taught by him, as the truth is in Jesus: that ye put off concerning the former conversation the old man, which is corrupt according to the deceitful lusts; and be renewed in the spirit of your mind; and that ye put on the new man, which after God is created in righteousness and true holiness.*

True holiness is here represented as having both a negative and a positive aspect. Speaking to those who had been disciples or learners in the school of Christ, Paul commands them to put off the old man and, being renewed inwardly, to put on the new man in righteousness and true holiness. The old man must go before the new man can come. The negative cleansing must precede the positive infilling. There is nothing here concerning toleration, counteraction, or suppression. The Word is clear: "Put off the old man."[3]

Eph. 5:25-27: *Husbands, love your wives, even as Christ also loved the church, and gave himself for it; that he might sanctify and cleanse it with the washing of water by the word, that he might present it to himself a glorious church, not having spot, or wrinkle, or any such thing; but that it should be holy and without blemish.*

This is the redemptive purpose of Christ for His Church. In relation to the world, divine love gave the Son to save from perishing those who believe. In relation to the Church, divine love gave the Son to sanctify and cleanse it, that it might be presented holy and without blame. There is an equation here of sanctification and cleansing. The Church cannot be presented without spot or wrinkle unless she first be sanctified and cleansed.

Titus 2:14: *Who gave himself for us, that he might redeem us from all iniquity, and purify unto himself a peculiar people, zealous of good works.* The atonement here is spoken of as having for its purpose "purifying unto himself" a people. This is a purity which is real and experiential, and which results in a zeal for good works. As is true in so many references, the inner experience is said to produce outer results, and the outer results certify the reality of the inward experience.

I John 1:7-8: *If we walk in the light, as he is in the light, we have fellowship one with another, and the blood of Jesus Christ his Son cleanseth us from all sin. If we say that we have no sin, we deceive ourselves, and the truth is not in us.*

Next to Romans 7, I John 1:8 is probably the verse quoted most frequently in the effort to contradict the Wesleyan claim to freedom from the inbeing of sin. Lewis Sperry Chafer, for example, proposes to disprove what he calls "the eradication error" by such an appeal as follows:

> The New Testament warns specifically against the eradication error. In I John 1:8 it is said, "If we say that we have no sin, we deceive ourselves, and the truth is not in us." Reference here is to a sin nature, whereas in verse 10 reference is to sin which is the fruit of the evil nature. To say as an assumption that one does not have a sin nature may be due to self-deception; nevertheless, to such it is declared: "The truth is not in him."[4]

Only by taking verse 8 completely out of context could it support such a conclusion. In verse 7, John indicates the need of walking in the light as God is Light, so that the Blood can cleanse from all sin. For if anyone alleges he has no sin from which he can and needs to be cleansed, the truth is not in him—he is self-deceived. Many indeed are the errors that could be avoided by applying to each verse of scripture the warning often printed on the tickets we buy: "Not good if detached." Here, as always, "A text without a context is only a pretext!"

This, then, is the testimony of Scripture. It stands squarely on the side of the actual cleansing of the heart of the believer, as against an imputed holiness which leaves the nature untouched. If God does not cleanse the hearts of His children, it would, of logical necessity, be for one of two reasons: either He *could* not do so; or, if He could, He *would* not do so. What a strange dilemma this would raise! If God wants to make His people actually holy and cannot, He is not omnipotent—the devil has succeeded in injecting into human nature that which God cannot remove. On the other hand, if God can cleanse the heart and will not, then He is not holy as we have thought Him to be, utterly opposed to all sin.

Why grapple with such perplexities? Why not take one's stand with the Bible and a multitude of witnesses, and proclaim the truth that God both *can* and *will* sanctify wholly every entirely converted child of His who will "receive the promise of the Spirit through faith" (Gal. 3:14)?

Chapter 2

PROCESS AND CRISIS
IN SANCTIFICATION

The second current issue in holiness teaching we shall consider has to do with the temporal aspect of sanctification. Does this experience result from growth and self-discipline, or is it an act of God's grace completed in a moment of time?

The concept of positional sanctification considered in Chapter 1 is usually reinforced with two closely related assertions: (1) that experimental (experiential) sanctification is progressive and gradual; and (2) that it is completed only at or after death in the gathering of the saints in glory.

These two points were evident in the quotation from Scofield given in Chapter 1, and are treated at greater length in the following quotation from Lewis Sperry Chafer in his *Systematic Theology*. After describing what he calls "positional sanctification," Chafer continues:

> Second, experimental sanctification. This second aspect of the sanctifying work of God for the believer is *progressive* in some of its aspects, so is quite in contrast to the *positional* sanctification which is "once for all." It is accomplished by the power of God through the Spirit and through the Word: "Sanctify them through thy truth: thy word is truth" (John 17:17; see also II Cor. 3:18; Eph. 5:25-26; I Thess. 5:23; II Pet. 3:18). Experimental sanctification is advanced according to various relationships. (1) In relation to the believer's yieldedness to God. In virtue of presenting his body a living sacrifice, the child of God thereby is set apart unto God and so is experimentally sanctified. The presentation may be ab-

solute and thus admit of no progression, or it may be partial and so require a further development. In either case, it is a work of experimental sanctification. (2) In relation to sin. The child of God may so comply with every condition for true spirituality as to be experiencing all the provided deliverance and victory from the power of sin, or, on the other hand, he may be experiencing but a partial deliverance from the power of sin. In either case, he is set apart and thus is experimentally sanctified. (3) In relation to Christian growth. This aspect of experimental sanctification is progressive in every case. It therefore should in no way be confused with incomplete yieldedness to God or incomplete victory over sin. Its meaning is that the knowledge of truth, devotion, and Christian experience are naturally subject to development. In accord with their present state of development as Christians, believers experimentally are set apart unto God. And thus, again, the Christian is subject to an experimental sanctification which is progressive. . . . The Bible, therefore, does not teach that any child of God is altogether sanctified experimentally in daily life before that final consummation of all things.[1]

There is much in this quotation concerning growth in grace with which we have no quarrel. Our question concerns calling this "sanctification," and the assertion that experimental sanctification cannot therefore be completed. Other writers in similar vein add the idea that the sin nature may be progressively brought under control, mortified daily by careful attention to the means of grace, and that thereby the believer is being progressively sanctified by gaining greater and greater victory over sin in his life, and more and more control over the impulses of sin in his heart.

This puts the issue squarely before us. Entire sanctification, as understood by holiness people, does not admit of degrees. It is as perfect and complete in its kind as the work of regeneration and justification is perfect and complete in its kind. This does not mean that there is no growth in grace both before and after sanctification. What it does mean is that sanctification, as an act of God, is instantaneous and not produced by growth or self-discipline or the progressive control of the carnal nature.

SANCTIFICATION BY GROWTH

Before asking, "What saith the Lord?" let us give momentary consideration to the growth theory.

First, it is difficult to see in this anything more than sanctification by works and human striving. The help of the Holy Spirit is claimed while the possibility of His dispensational work is denied. It is possible to give lip service to the Spirit's ministry and at the same time to contradict His sanctifying lordship.

Second, death is expected to complete what grace and the cross of Christ could not. Lurking back of all these speculations is the ghost of the ancient Gnostic heresy, that the physical body is in some sense the seat and source of sin. There is otherwise no logical reason for such persistent doubt that the redeemed soul may be free from sin here and now.

More crucial still is the fact that the Bible never intimates anywhere that either growth or death have the least thing to do with the soul's sanctification. Instead, the Word of God, the blood of Christ, the Holy Spirit, and faith are factors concerned with sanctification. Growth is *in* grace, never *into* grace. Growth relates to increase in *quantity*, never to change in *quality*. Further, to suppose that physical death makes any change in the moral quality of the human soul is to go in direct opposition to the clear statements of the Word (Heb. 9:27; Rev. 22:11).

SANCTIFICATION AS A CRISIS EXPERIENCE

As we turn to the testimony of the Word, we find three classes of evidence that entire sanctification is, in fact, instantaneous and not gradual, a crisis experience and not an endless process. There is, first, the analogy to justification and the new birth. Second, there is the testimony of the terms used to describe the work—terms which customarily refer to actions completed at a given point in time. And, third, there is the logic of example found in the Bible. Let us look briefly at each.

1. · *The Analogy with the New Birth*

There are several points of similarity between the two works of divine grace: justification or the new birth, and sanctification or holiness.

a. Both are products of divine love. John 3:16 reads: *For God so loved the world, that he gave his only begotten Son, that whosoever believeth in him should not perish, but have everlasting life;* and Eph. 5:25-27 says: *Husbands, love your wives, even as Christ also loved the church, and gave himself for it; that he might sanctify and cleanse it with the washing of water by the word . . . that it should be holy and without blemish.*

b. Both are manifestations of God's good, acceptable, and perfect will. I Tim. 2:3-4 says: *For this is good and acceptable in the sight of God our Saviour; who will have all men to be saved, and to come unto the knowledge of the truth;* and Heb. 10:10: *By the which will* (that is, the will of God as accomplished by Christ in His atoning death) *we are sanctified through the offering of the body of Jesus Christ once for all.*

c. Both are accomplished through the wonderful light of God's Word. I Pet. 1:23 reads: *Being born again, not of corruptible seed, but of incorruptible, by the word of God, which liveth and abideth for ever;* and in John 17:17 Christ's prayer is: *Sanctify them through thy truth: thy word is truth.*

d. Both are wrought in the heart by the effective agency of the Holy Spirit of God. Titus 3:5 says: *Not by works of righteousness which we have done, but according to his*

mercy he saved us, by the washing of regeneration, and re-
newing of the Holy Ghost; and II Thess. 2:13 reads: *But we
are bound to give thanks to God always for you, brethren
beloved of the Lord, because God hath from the beginning
chosen you to salvation through sanctification of the Spirit
and belief of the truth.*

e. Both are purchased at the cost of Christ's shed blood
on Calvary's cross. In Rom. 5:9, Paul says: *Much more
then, being now justified by his blood, we shall be saved
from wrath through him;* and Heb. 13:12 reads: *Wherefore
Jesus also, that he might sanctify the people with his own
blood, suffered without the gate.*

f. Both are brought to the individual believer's heart in
response to faith. Rom. 5:1 reads: *Therefore being justified
by faith, we have peace with God through our Lord Jesus
Christ;* and Acts 26:18, *To open their eyes, and to turn them
from darkness to light, and from the power of Satan unto
God, that they may receive the forgiveness of sins, and inheritance among them which are sanctified by faith that is
in me.*

Now virtually all evangelical Christians recognize that
the new birth, justification, is not gradual but instantaneous.
It is an act of God which takes place at a given point in a believer's life. But if both justification and sanctification are
products of the same divine love, the same will of God, the
same Holy Word, the same blessed Spirit, the same redeem-
ing Blood, and the same human condition—namely, faith—
is there any valid reason for supposing that one is
instantaneous while the other is gradual? If justification is
instantaneous, there is certainly no reason why sanctification, wrought by the same agency, should not be equally the
act of a moment.

As a matter of fact, every argument which proves the
instantaneousness of regeneration is just as forceful when
applied to sanctification. Conversely, if the evidence for the

immediacy of sanctification be rejected, there is no logical ground on which to base proof for the immediacy of justification.

2. *The Testimony of the Terms*

Without exception, the root action in the terms used to describe sanctification implies that which occurs at a particular point in time.

a. The verb "to sanctify" is defined in its twofold meaning as "to set apart" and "to make holy." There may, it is true, be a gradual setting apart, a gradual making holy. But the action described is much more naturally thought of as momentary and immediate. Since "to sanctify" in its strictly New Testament sense is always spoken of as a divine act, the burden of proof ought naturally to rest upon those who allege sanctification to be gradual.

b. Then, this experience is spoken of as a baptism: *John truly baptized with water, but ye shall be baptized with the Holy Ghost not many days hence* (Acts 1:5).[2] Baptism is a term which always implies action at a given point—never that which is drawn out over a period of time, and perhaps never completed until death. Gradual baptism is an absurdity—whether it be a baptism with water or the baptism with the Holy Spirit.

c. Sanctification is also spoken of as a crucifixion or death. Rom. 6:6 reads: *Knowing this, that our old man is crucified with him, that the body of sin might be destroyed, that henceforth we should not serve sin;* Gal. 2:20: *I am crucified with Christ: nevertheless I live; yet not I, but Christ liveth in me: and the life which I now live in the flesh, I live by the faith of the Son of God, who loved me, and gave himself for me;* and Col 3:5, *Mortify* (treat as dead) *therefore your members which are upon the earth.*

Granted that one may be long a-dying, but death always occurs in a moment. Life may wane over a period of time, but it departs the body at a given instant. Gradual death is a figure of speech for a mortal illness. Death itself is always instantaneous.

d. Sanctification, furthermore, involves cleansing or purifying. The verses quoted in Chapter 1 are replete with uses of the verb forms of these words. Cleansing and purification may be continuous processes, but the natural meaning of these words indicates that there is always an initial moment when the cleansing and purification is first accomplished. To make it gradual is to read into it something which the words themselves do not imply.

e. This experience is also described as a "gift" to be "received." "The gift of the Holy Ghost" is frequently mentioned throughout the New Testament, often as "the promise of the Father." Jesus, in Luke 11:13, said, *If ye then, being evil, know how to give good gifts unto your children: how much more shall your heavenly Father give the Holy Spirit to them that ask him?* Gal. 3:14 reads: *That we might receive the promise of the Spirit through faith.* Is it not obvious that a gift is something which passes into the possession of its receiver at some given moment? The gradual giving of a gift is a confusion of terms.

We could go on at length. Sanctification is variously described as putting off the old man and putting on the new (Eph. 4:20-24); it is destroying the body of sin (Rom. 6:6); it is being filled with the Spirit (Eph. 5:18); it is to be sealed with that Holy Spirit of promise (Eph. 1:13).

To summarize: "to set apart," "to make holy," "to baptize," "to crucify," "to put to death," "to give," "to receive," "to put off," "to put on," "to destroy," "to be filled," "to be sealed"—these are all verbs describing actions which take place most naturally at a definite time and place, and which do not admit of degrees. They all testify to the fact that sanctification is a crisis experience, not a long-drawn-out and never-completed process of growth.

3. The Logic of Example

The experience of Isaiah recorded in Isaiah 6 may be regarded as a type of the believer's experience of entire sanctification. Isaiah had been a prophet of God during part of the reign of King Uzziah, as he tells us in chapter 1. But it was in the year the king died that God's prophet experienced his remarkable cleansing.

In the Temple worshiping, Isaiah saw the Lord "high and lifted up," and heard the seraphs' song, *Holy, holy, holy, is the Lord of hosts.* That praise of God's holiness found no echo in the prophet's heart, and he who had previously called woes on the people now cried out again for himself, *Woe is me! for I am undone; because I am a man of unclean lips, and I dwell in the midst of a people of unclean lips.*

But the divine response was not long in coming. An angel flew with golden tongs and a live coal from the altar, touched his lips, and said, *Lo, this hath touched thy lips; and thine iniquity is taken away, and thy sin purged.* This all took place in less time than it takes to describe. It was not by growth or spiritual development that Isaiah's iniquity was taken away and his sin purged. It was by divine act at a given time.

In the New Testament, all examples of the baptism with the Spirit and entire sanctification are found in the Book of Acts.[3] They are four in number.

a. The first involves the disciples of Jesus, whose names were written in heaven (Luke 10:20); who were not of the world (John 14:16-17; 17:14); who belonged to Christ (John 17:6, 11); not one of whom was lost (John 17:12); and who had kept God's words (John 17:6). While these clearly justified persons *were all with one accord in one place . . . suddenly there came a sound from heaven as of a rushing mighty wind . . . And they were all filled with the Holy Ghost"* (Acts 2:1-4). There was no gradual growing

29

into this. It came with the unexpected suddenness of lightning from the skies.

b. The second example found in the Book of Acts was the young church in Samaria. Philip had ventured into Samaria after the martyrdom of Stephen. His preaching met with a ready response. The people believed and were baptized in large numbers. Acts 8:8 records that "there was great joy in that city."

Hearing of this revival and the success of the ministry of the Word, the apostles at Jerusalem sent Peter and John to Samaria. When they came, they prayed for these young converts *that they might receive the Holy Ghost: (for as yet he was fallen upon none of them: only they were baptized in the name of the Lord Jesus). Then laid they their hands on them, and they received the Holy Ghost* (Acts 8:15-17).

It is sometimes fashionable to reject the example of the disciples of Christ as not truly typical because they lived under two dispensations. Thus, it is claimed, Pentecost was in effect the completion of their regeneration, and every believer now receives the baptism with the Holy Spirit at the moment he first receives Christ as his Saviour. This argument is refuted by the example of the Samaritan church. The Samaritans believed and were baptized in the new dispensation of the Spirit, and they were afterwards filled with the Holy Ghost at a given instant of time.

c. The third example concerns the devout Roman centurion Cornelius, and members of his household. Cornelius is described in clear terms by God's inspired penman. He was a devout man (Acts 10:2); he feared God with all his house (Acts 10:2); he prayed constantly, and his prayers were accepted by God (Acts 10:2, 4). Peter, arriving at Cornelius' house, with quick spiritual insight said: *Of a truth, I perceive that God is no respecter of persons, but in every nation he that feareth him, and worketh righteousness, is accepted with him. The word which God sent unto*

30

the children of Israel, preaching peace by Jesus Christ: (he is Lord of all:) that word, I say, ye know, which was published throughout all Judaea (Acts 10:34-37).

As Peter continued to speak, suddenly the Holy Spirit fell on those who listened. This was not gradual, but instantaneous. That Peter himself regarded the events at Cornelius' home as identical to the events at Pentecost is clearly seen in his report to the council at Jerusalem: God, knowing their hearts, bore witness and gave the Holy Spirit, even as He had at Pentecost, purifying their hearts by faith (Acts 15:8-9).[4]

d. The fourth instance given in the Book of Acts is described in 18:24 to 19:7. It concerns the disciples at Ephesus. Because there has been so much misunderstanding connected with this episode, it is necessary to go into the background a bit more extensively.

At the end of the Apostle Paul's long ministry in Corinth, he, in company with Aquila and Priscilla, his co-laborers, crossed the Aegean Sea to the mainland of Asia and the city of Ephesus. Paul himself spent only a brief time preaching in the synagogue at Ephesus. Leaving Aquila and Priscilla there, he went on toward Antioch.

While Paul was gone, a man named Apollos came to Ephesus. Apollos is described as eloquent, mighty in the Scriptures, instructed in the way of the Lord, and speaking and teaching diligently the things of the Lord, although, as far as baptism was concerned, he knew only the baptism of John. Recognizing the potential greatness of Apollos' ministry, Aquila and Priscilla took him and taught him the way of God more perfectly (Acts 18:24-28).

Shortly after Apollos left his newfound friends to go to Corinth, Paul came back to Ephesus. Whatever their origin, whether as converts of Aquila and Priscilla, or of Apollos, Paul found in Ephesus a nucleus of 12 disciples. Examining them, he learned that they had not received the Holy

31

Ghost, at least in the measure of Pentecost. But after Paul had baptized them in the name of Christ, he prayed, laid hands upon them, and they were filled with the Holy Spirit.

The misunderstanding which surrounds this incident has to do with the spiritual status of the Ephesian disciples. Because they disclaimed knowledge of the Holy Spirit, and because they had received only the baptism of John, some have contended that they were unregenerate persons. But there is strong evidence that these 12 people were genuine children of God, and that this was for them a second instantaneous experience. Let us examine the important considerations here.

(1) The men are described as disciples (Acts 19:1). Relate this to Acts 11:26: *The disciples were called Christians first in Antioch.* The designations "Christian" and "disciple" were used interchangeably in the Book of Acts. There is no instance of the use of the term "disciple" in the Acts for any other than true believers in Christ.

(2) Paul did not challenge the fact of their faith. *Have ye received the Holy Ghost since ye believed?* he asked them (Acts 19:2). Whether the original be translated as it is thus in the Authorized Version, or translated as it is in the American Standard Version and Revised Standard Version, *Did you receive the Holy Spirit when you believed?* makes not the slightest bit of difference so far as this point is concerned. In either case, it is admitted that they had believed, and it is evident that they had not received the Holy Ghost in the sense in which Paul speaks.

(3) That they were ignorant of the receiving of the Holy Spirit does not mean that they had not been converted. Dwight L. Moody asserted that for many years after his conversion he did not know that the Holy Spirit was a Person, and that many believers today are as ignorant of the person and ministry of the Holy Spirit as were these Ephesian believers.[5]

(4) That these men had only the baptism of John does not prove that they were unconverted in the full Christian sense of the word. The baptism of John is spoken of as a "baptism of repentance for the remission of sins" (Mark 1:4). Apollos, instructed in the way of the Lord, fervent in the Spirit, speaking and teaching diligently the things of the Lord, knew only the baptism of John.

(5) That Paul was satisfied with the faith of these disciples is seen in the fact that he rebaptized them in the name of the Lord Jesus Christ before they were filled with the Holy Spirit. If they were only at that time being regenerated in the Christian sense, then Paul was guilty of baptizing a group of unconverted men. That such has often been done since, we will not debate; but that Paul began the practice in Ephesus, we cannot admit.

(6) That "receiving" the Holy Spirit refers to something more than being born again by the Spirit and led by the Spirit is testified to by no less authority than the Lord Jesus himself. In John 14:15-17, we read: *If ye love me, keep my commandments. And I will pray the Father, and he shall give you another Comforter, that he may abide with you for ever; even the Spirit of truth; whom the world cannot receive, because it seeth him not, neither knoweth him: but ye know him; for he dwelleth with you, and shall be in you.*

Here Jesus indicates clearly that the world, and those who are of the world, cannot receive the Holy Spirit. One must *know* Him before *receiving* Him. One must have the Spirit *with* him before he can have the Spirit *in* him. While the phrase "receive the Holy Spirit" is used only four times in the New Testament (John 14:17; Acts 8:15-17; Acts 19:2; and Gal. 3:14), in each case it is made clear that it is the believer alone who is in a position to *receive* Him. We should not put too much weight on the analogy, but it is surely no accident that the inspired writers of the New Testament chose the figures *birth of the Spirit* to represent regeneration, and *baptism with the Spirit* to describe the "second blessing." Obviously, in the order of nature, birth *must* precede baptism—a child has to be born before he can be baptized.

Here then is the logic of example. Each instance was characterized by immediacy. Each took place at a given point in the experience of the persons involved. Nowhere is there a trace of sanctification by growth, a long process of self-discipline, never completed until the rapture. If sanctification is of faith, then it is "not of works, lest any man should boast" (Rom. 11:6, Eph. 2:9).

THE TESTIMONY OF THE TENSES

There is another impressive line of evidence for the instantaneousness of sanctification that is of particular interest to one who has some acquaintance with Greek grammar. A most persuasive summary of this argument is to be found in the article by Dr. Daniel Steele, included in his *Milestone Papers*, entitled "The Tense Readings of the Greek New Testament."[6]

The main point in this argument lies in the fact that the tenses of the Greek verb have a somewhat different meaning from those of the English. Our verb tenses have to do mainly with the *time* of action—past, present, or future. Greek tenses do denote time, but more particularly they indicate the *kind* of action. Action may be viewed as a continuing process, known as *linear* action; or it may be viewed as a whole in what is known as momentary or *punctiliar* action. Continued action or a state of incompleteness is denoted by the present and imperfect tenses in the Greek. On the other hand, point-action, that which is momentary or punctiliar, is expressed by the consistent use of the aorist tense. William Hersey Davis says, *"The aorist tense itself always means point-action."*[7]

The aorist refers to actions "thought of merely as events or single facts without reference to the time they occupied."[8] With the exception of the indicative aorist, which denotes past action, aorist forms are undefined as to time. They all represent punctiliar as opposed to linear action. They describe completed, epochal events, treated as a totality. The aorist, says Alford, implies a definite act.[9]

The relevance of all this to our present subject is seen in the following quotation from Dr. Steele in the paper referred to earlier. Speaking of the findings of his study of the use of verb tenses in key New Testament passages, he says:

1. All exhortations to prayer and to spiritual endeavor in resistance of temptation are usually expressed in the present tense, which strongly indicates persistence. . . .

2. The next fact which impresses us in our investigation is *the absence of the aorist and the presence of the present tense whenever the conditions of final salvation are stated.* Our inference is that the conditions of ultimate salvation are continuous, extending through probation, and not completed in any one act. The great requirement is faith in Jesus Christ. A careful study of the Greek will convince the student that it is a great mistake to teach that a single act of faith furnishes a person with a paid-up, non-forfeitable policy assuring the holder that he will inherit eternal life, or that a single energy of faith secures a through ticket for heaven, as is taught by the Plymouth Brethren and by some popular lay evangelists. The Greek tenses show that faith is a state, a habit of mind, into which the believer enters at justification. . . .

3. But when we come to consider the *work of purification* in the believer's soul, by the power of the Holy Spirit, both in the new birth and in entire sanctification, we find that *the aorist is almost uniformly used.* This tense, according to the best New Testament grammarians, never indicates a continuous, habitual, or repeated act, but one which is momentary, and done once for all.[10]

We have looked in vain to find one of these verbs (denoting sanctification and perfection) in the imperfect tense when individuals are spoken of. The verb *hagiazo,* to sanctify, is always aorist or perfect. . . . The same may be said of the verbs *katharizo* and *hagnizo*, to purify. Our inference is that the energy of the Holy Spirit in the work of entire sanctification, however long the preparation, is put forth at a stroke by a momentary act. This is corroborated by the universal testimony of those who have experienced this grace.[11]

It was Dr. E. F. Walker who pointed out years ago that, in the final analysis, all theories of sanctification must recognize its instantaneousness. If sanctification is at physical death, or at the resurrection, it must occur in an instant. Even if it be by growth, there must be a precise time when full growth is attained. The debate centers about the issue as to when that completing instant occurs.

Here, we affirm, the testimony of God's Word is final. The hour of full salvation is not some remote future hour. The day of deliverance from all indwelling sin is not some far-off day. Every divine imperative, every command of God is for the present moment, never for the future. *Behold, now is the accepted time; behold, now is the day of salvation* (II Cor. 6:2).

Chapter 3

CHRISTIAN PERFECTION AND SIN

One of the most important issues emerging in modern evangelical circles is the definition of sin. It is more than a theoretical argument over the proper usage of terms. It goes directly to the heart of Christian life and experience. It has bearing on every branch of the doctrine of salvation. Our conception of the whole plan of redemption is radically affected thereby. As Richard S. Taylor has conclusively shown in his book *A Right Conception of Sin*,[1] the concept of sin is fundamental in Christian thought.

It is not our purpose here to consider the entire problem. We will suggest first a crucial test which may be applied to the definition of sin—or any other definition for that matter—and hence arrive at an accurate statement of what the term means. We shall then point out the bearing of the accepted definition on the doctrine of entire sanctification.

THE MEANING OF "SIN"

What is the proper, New Testament sense of the verb "to sin"? Does it mean, as is often said, to deviate in any particular from an absolute and objective standard of perfect righteousness? Or does the essence of sin consist in a wrong intent, an impure motive? Without necessarily prejudicing the case, we may, for convenience, call the former view the *legal* concept of sin, and the latter view the *ethical* concept. The two lead in radically different directions.

There are, as is well known, two major uses of the term sin and its related terms in the Bible. These are roughly indicated by the part of speech involved. *Sin* is used as a noun, and in the singular form it usually describes a nature, a state of character, an aspect of being. Such is the usage found, for example, in the sixth chapter of Romans: *Sin shall not have dominion over you: for ye are not under the law, but under grace* (v. 14); and, *Now being made free from sin, and become servants to God, ye have your fruit unto holiness, and the end everlasting life* (v. 22).

Again, *sin* is used as a verb, to denote a kind of action, a mode of behavior. Since the noun forms are derived from the verb, and since it is with the nature of sinful actions that we are concerned here, we shall confine our attention for the present to the verb "to sin," and endeavor to learn the sort of conduct to which it refers.

The most frequently used Greek verb for sinful action in the New Testament is *hamartano*, traditionally defined as "to miss the mark." So far as the root meaning of the Greek term goes, we get little light on its scriptural usage. There is no indication as to what mark is missed, or as to why and how it is missed. An archer may fail by reason of shooting at the wrong mark, by reason of carelessness in taking aim, because he is too weak to draw the bowstring back far enough, or merely because he is a poor shot.

There is little promise of help, then, in a study of the derivation or etymology of the term. We must shape and verify our definition on other grounds than what the original term meant.

Sin is often defined as "any violation of, or want of conformity to, the perfect will of God." Chafer states that the believer, searching his life for sin, should ask, "Have I done *all* and *only* His will with motives as pure as heaven and in the unchanging faithfulness of manner characterizing the Infinite?"[2] If that is the criterion, none of us have far to search. What finite creature can live in "the unchanging faithfulness of manner characterizing the Infinite"?

This point of view would judge all behavior objectively, as it relates to an abstract law of perfect righteousness. Sin is then defined as any deviation, whatever its occasion or cause, from this absolute standard. Since no finite creature can escape such failures, it is concluded that to be human is to be liable to sin "every day, in word, thought, and deed."

Arminian theologians have generally been willing to concede this so-called "broad" definition of sin. They have immediately set up in opposition to it, however, a "narrow" definition which understands sin to be "the willful transgression of a known law of God." This John Wesley does in a famous passage in *A Plain Account of Christian Perfection:*

> The best of men still need Christ in His priestly office, to atone for their omissions, their shortcomings (as some not improperly speak), their mistakes in judgment and practice, and their defects of various kinds. For these are all deviations from the perfect law, and consequently need an atonement. Yet that they are not properly sins, we apprehend may appear from the words of St. Paul, "He that loveth hath fulfilled the law; for love is the fulfilling of the law" (Rom. 13:10). Now mistakes, and whatever infirmities necessarily flow from the corruptible state of the body, are no way contrary to love; nor, therefore, in the Scripture sense, sin. . . .
>
> Not only sin, properly so-called (that is, a voluntary transgression of a known law), but sin, improperly so-called (that is, an involuntary transgression of a Divine law, known or unknown), needs atoning blood. I believe there is no such perfection in this life as excludes these involuntary transgressions, which I apprehend to be naturally consequent on the ignorance and mistakes inseparable from mortality. Therefore, *sinless perfection* is a phrase I never use, lest I should seem to contradict

myself. I believe, a person filled with the love of God is still liable to involuntary transgressions.[3]

Without ignoring the "broad" definition, Wesley's second insight is truer to the New Testament concept of sin. Sin, in the New Testament, is an ethical and not a legal concept. As such, it must involve both knowledge or light, and choice or motive.

All this becomes of prime importance when we turn to the question of the believer's deliverance from sin. The legal or "broad" definition of sin necessarily includes the ethical or "narrow" definition. The question is, Can a Christian live a life which is free from sin? Here, as ever, we have no better standard than the Word of God.

On Testing a Definition

The fundamental principle involved in the discussion of the next few pages may be quite simply stated as follows: The sense in which a term is used can be determined only by putting the definition for the term in the context in which it occurs. If the total passage makes good sense when the proposed definition is substituted for the term in question, then the definition is a satisfactory one. If the passage becomes false or meaningless when the proposed definition is substituted for the term in question, then the definition must be regarded as unsatisfactory.

To illustrate: We are all familiar with the proverbial saying, "The exception proves the rule." Now the verb "to prove" has two definitions. It may be defined as "to establish the truth of," but it may also be defined as "to test or try the truth of." We prove a geometrical proposition in the first sense; in the second sense, we have proving grounds such as at Aberdeen where army artillery may be tested.

What is the meaning of the verb "to prove" in the proverb, "The exception proves the rule"? Try the substitution of the first definition: "The exception establishes the truth of the rule." This is obviously self-contradictory. In this context, definition number one becomes meaningless. Try substitution of the second definition: "The exception tests or tries the truth of the rule." This is obviously meaningful and true, and establishes the second definition as the one which best expresses the meaning of the term in question.

This is what we propose as a method of determining precisely the New Testament meaning of the verb "to sin." Let us state the two opposing definitions as concisely as possible. Then let us substitute each in turn for the verb where it is used in the New Testament (41 places in all).[4] In this way we shall be able to determine which definition comes nearest to embodying the New Testament concept of *hamartano*, "to sin."

Since limitations of space forbid a study of all 41 verses, we shall first give a summary of findings from a complete examination of all passages, and then present several representative examples.

The legal definition of sin may be stated briefly, "To deviate in any manner from an absolute standard of perfect behavior." The ethical definition may be given in Wesley's clipped phrase, "To wilfully transgress the known law of God."

Making the substitution in each of the 41 references[5] we obtain some very interesting results. The ethical definition will fit and make sense in all of them without exception. The legal definition will make sense in *only four* of them. It cannot be substituted in any of the remaining 37 without incoherence or self-contradiction.

That the legal definition—"to deviate in any manner from an absolute standard of perfect behavior"—*does* make sense in four of the passages *does not* of itself mean that it is therefore the proper definition even for these passages. This is because the ethical definition makes even better sense in these same passages, and has the immeasurably greater advantage of being consistent with the rest of the New Testament.

Let us look briefly at the four uses in which either definition will fit. They are found in Rom. 2:12, where the verb is used twice; in Rom. 3:23; and in I John 1:10. These references read as follows: *For as many as have sinned without law shall also perish without law: and as many as have sinned in the law shall be judged by the law; For all have sinned, and come short of the glory of God; and, If we say that we have not sinned, we make him a liar, and his word is not in us.*

As previously stated, we *could* read these verses with the legal definition in place of the word, and make a passing degree of sense. We could read, "As many as have *deviated in any manner from an absolute standard of perfect behavior* without law shall also perish without law: and as many as have *deviated from an absolute standard* in the law shall be judged by the law"; "For all have *deviated from an absolute standard of perfect behavior,* and come short of the glory of God"; "If we say we have not *deviated from an absolute standard of perfect behavior,* we make him a liar, and his word is not in us."

However, notice how much more natural and more meaningful is the ethical definition in these same passages. "As many as have *willfully transgressed the known requirement of God* without law[6] shall also perish without law: and as many as have *transgressed the known law of God* in the law shall by judged by the law"; "For all have *willfully transgressed the known law of God,* and come short of His glory"; "If we say we have not *willfully transgressed God's known law,* we make him a liar, and his word is not in us."

42

The decisive verses are those 37 in which the legal definition will not fit. No definition can possibly be accepted as satisfactory which destroys the meaning of 90 percent of the passages in which the term occurs. For purposes of illustration, the following five have been arbitrarily selected:

1. In John 5:14, we read: *Afterward Jesus findeth him in the temple, and said unto him, Behold, thou art made whole: sin no more, lest a worse thing come unto thee.* Substituting the legal definition we would read: "Behold, thou art made whole: *deviate no more in any manner from an absolute standard of perfect behavior*, lest a worse thing come unto thee." This would certainly place the poor fellow in a terrible spot! How could he avoid all deviations from a perfect standard, known or unknown, voluntary or involuntary? But when we insert the ethical definition of sin, our Lord's requirement becomes reasonable and, by His grace, possible: "Behold, thou art made whole: *willfully transgress* no more *the known law of God*, lest a worse thing come unto thee."

2. Next, we test Rom. 6:15: *What then? shall we sin, because we are not under the law, but under grace? God forbid.* Substituting the legal definition we are confronted with this patent absurdity: "What then? shall we *deviate in any manner from an absolute standard of perfect righteousness*, because we are not under the law, but under grace? God forbid." However, the ethical definition places before us the New Testament standard of Christian conduct: "What then? shall we *willfully transgress the known law of God* because we are not under the law, but under grace? God forbid."

3. Another from the Pauline Epistles is I Cor. 15:34: *Awake to righteousness, and sin not; for some have not the knowledge of God: I speak this to your shame.* Inserting the legal definition, we would have, "Awake to righteousness,

and never *deviate in any manner from an absolute standard of perfect behavior;* for some have not the knowledge of God." Since those who hold this definition deny the possibility of living without sin in word, thought, or deed any day, this makes the verse an absurdity. However, the ethical definition reveals this as the universal obligation of all New Testament believers: "Awake to righteousness, and never *willfully transgress the known law of God;* for some have not the knowledge of God."

4. A fourth test verse is found in Heb. 10:26, a solemn verse which warns that Christ's atonement does not avail for those living in willful sin. It reads: "For if we sin will-fully after that we have received the knowledge of the truth, there remaineth no more sacrifice for sin." The presence of the adjective "willfully," which highlights the deliberate character of the sin under question, makes it difficult to make our substitution. However, it would result in something like the following: "For if we *deviate in any manner from an absolute standard of perfect behavior,* after that we have received the knowledge of the truth, there remaineth no more sacrifice for sins." This would be enough to bring despair to anyone.

But suppose we read it with the ethical definition of sin: "For if we deliberately and *willfully transgress God's known law,* after that we have received the knowledge of the truth, there remaineth no more sacrifice for sins." This is a solemn warning, but one in perfect harmony with the whole tenor of the New Testament. It is not meant to take hope from the backslider, but to warn all—regardless of previous standing in grace—that no one can live in willful and known sin and rightly claim the efficacy of Christ's atoning death. An examination of the original here reveals the participial form of the verb—"Sinning willfully, there remaineth no more sacrifice for sin." When the backslider turns again to God in sincere repentance, he finds a perfect adequacy in the atoning Blood as a sacrifice for sins.

5. Our last test passage is I John 3:8-9. Here we read: *He that committeth sin is of the devil, for the devil sinneth from the beginning. For this purpose the Son of God was manifested, that he might destroy the works of the devil. Whosoever is born of God doth not commit sin; for his seed remaineth in him: and he cannot sin, because he is born of God.* Two of the terms here are nouns, and two are verbs. However, the coherence of the passage demands that they be understood as bearing the same meaning.

Let us first test the legal definition. The verses in question would then read: "He who *deviates in any manner from an absolute standard of perfect righteousness* is of the devil; for the devil *so deviates* from the beginning. . . .* Whosoever is born of God does not *deviate from absolute righteousness;* for his seed remaineth in him: and he cannot *so deviate,* because he is born of God." This would drastically limit the number of the children of God. It would eliminate all finite human beings, for sure.

When we turn to the ethical definition, and recognize the verb forms as those used of repeated and customary action, we find in these verses consistency with the whole of God's revealed truth. "He who is *willfully violating the known law of God* is of the devil; for the devil *so violates God's law* from the beginning. . . . Whosoever is born of God is not *willfully violating God's known law;* for his seed remaineth in him: and he cannot be *willfully violating God's known law,* because he is born of God."

Some have tried to turn the force of this verse by interpreting the words "he cannot sin" to mean "he is not able to sin." It should be pointed out, however, that "cannot" is here used in a logical and legislative sense, and not to indicate inability.

For example, we may paraphrase this verse and thus see its whole meaning as follows: "Whosoever is an honest man does not steal; for his honesty remaineth in him; and he cannot steal because he is an honest man." This makes perfect sense. It does not mean that an honest man is incapable of taking that which does not belong to him. He has hands and feet and desires just like other men. What it does say is that an honest man *cannot* steal. It is logically impossible to be honest and a thief at the same time. When an honest man begins to steal, he ceases to be an honest man and becomes a thief.

Again, we may read, "Whosoever is a truthful man does not lie; for his truthfulness remaineth in him; and he cannot lie, because he is a truthful man." This too makes sense. It does not say that a truthful man lacks tongue and lips and mind wherewith to fabricate falsehoods. It does say that when a truthful man begins to lie, he is no longer truthful. He becomes a liar. Just as there is nowhere in God's universe an honest thief or a truthful liar, just so there is nowhere in God's universe a sinning saint, or a child of God living in willful violation of God's known law.

This does not mean that a sincere child of God may not, in a moment of spiritual weakness and under the stress of strong temptation, yield and commit sin. However, God has provided an instant remedy for this, as is shown in I John 2:1-2: *My little children, these things write I unto you, that ye sin not. And if any man sin, we have an advocate with the Father, Jesus Christ the righteous: and he is the propitiation for our sins; and not for ours only, but also for the sins of the whole world.*

Here the verbs are in the aorist tense, and indicate action not habitual and repeated. But even here, the lie is given to the idea that Christians cannot avoid sin. The admonition is written so that they will not sin. The normal course of conduct is "that ye sin not." The statement immediately following, "If any man sin," indicates that sin is the exception and not the rule. But when the tragedy occurs—and sin in the Christian life is nothing less—God has provided a remedy in an immediate confession and in the advocacy of "Jesus Christ the righteous." Not a moment must be lost in fleeing to the Blood, that its efficacy may be applied.

To fail to mend the breach immediately is to open the door to other sins, and to complete backsliding. Not the single, exceptional occurrence, immediately renounced and confessed, but the unrepentant persistence is what crushes out the spiritual life. A stranger asked an old fisherman on the dock,

"If one fell in here, would he drown?"

"Don't reckon he would," was the reply.

"Why, isn't the water deep enough?" queried the other.

"Plenty deep," the old native answered; "but 'tain't fallin' in, it's stayin' in, what drowns a feller."

To change the figure, when one has a flat tire on his automobile, that certainly does not represent the normal state of affairs. All cars are built to operate on four well-inflated tires. When the flat does come, there are two things which may be done. One can simply drive on to the next service station or garage—five, 10, or 15 miles down the road —to seek help. But by that time there would not be just a puncture to repair, but a new tube and/or tire to purchase, and maybe even a new wheel. Mechanical damage could have resulted that would necessitate a major overhaul to get the car back on the road again. On the other hand, one could stop immediately, fix the puncture or put on the spare, and proceed without damage.

Too many young Christians, trapped momentarily into sin, just keep on running on the flat, so to speak, until the next revival or camp meeting. They give up their faith and throw away their confidence, and by the time the next revival or camp meeting comes along, they have not only a puncture to fix but a new tube, tire, and wheel to buy. A major overhaul is required to get them back on the road again. How much better to stop immediately, ask and receive forgiveness, and go on uninjured with only a momentary interruption of fellowship with God!

Our testing of these two different definitions of sin leads us to the conclusion that the legal definition is generally inadmissible. The ethical definition stands up to the crucial test in each instance. Further, it becomes evident that the New Testament holds up a standard of Christian life in general and the sanctified life in particular which would find no place for sinful conduct.

THE IMPORTANCE OF A RIGHT CONCEPT OF SIN

Someone may ask at this juncture, "But what difference does it make what one means by *sin*? Isn't this just a debate about words? Why not call lapses of memory, errors of judgment, and imperfections of behavior caused by human infirmities, sins?"

The answer is threefold. First, in the words of Dr. H. Orton Wiley, "Calling that sin which is not sin, opens the door also to actual sinning." To accept the "broad" or legal definition of sin is to be forced to the admission that flesh-bound human beings cannot escape the thralldom of sin. And to make everything sin is, in effect, to make nothing sin. It is impossible to grade sins. If forgotten promises, faulty judgment, and human infirmities are sins, then there is no qualitative distinction open between such so-called sins and lying, theft, or immorality. The door then is wide open to sin of all sorts.

Second, the Christian consciousness and conscience assert that there is a crucial qualitative difference here. When judged by the law of objective right, there is no difference between a forgotten promise and a broken promise. When judged by the law of objective right, there is no difference

48

between a misstatement of fact made in ignorance and a lie. It is simply that something promised has not been performed and an untruth has been told.

But what a difference there is when judged subjectively! In the case of both the forgotten promise and the ignorant misstatement, there is regret—but not guilt. There is sorrow, but not sin. Lapses of memory and ignorance are regrettable, and should be avoided as far as possible. But they do not interrupt fellowship with God, nor bring condemnation to the Christian consciousness.

Conscience always finds the essence of sin in the realm of intent or motive. This is not in any sense to minimize the material or objective side of the moral law. It does not give license for well-meaning blundering. It does, however, recognize that sin is fundamentally a matter of choice, of intention, of purpose.

Third, this distinction is vital because it is scriptural. The Bible throughout recognizes the fact of faults and infirmities, and it distinguishes them sharply from sin. For example, Christ saves us from our sins (Matt. 1:21); He cleanses us from carnal sin (I John 1:7); but He sympathizes with and is touched with the feeling of our infirmities (Heb. 4:15). This represents a vital difference in attitude toward sin on the one hand—both inner and outer—and human frailties on the other.

Again, the Holy Spirit convicts of sins (John 16:8), frees us from carnality (Rom. 8:2), but helps us with our infirmities (Rom. 8:26). Forgiveness of sins and cleansing from sin are instantaneously wrought. Infirmities cannot be cured by a crisis experience, but must be met on the battlefield of life day after day, and overcome or sublimated with the Spirit's help.

The moral law itself is of such character that it can be kept only by those whose love and motives are pure, and not by outward conformity alone, however detailed such might be. This is clearly the import of Paul in Rom. 13:8-10: *Owe no man any thing, but to love one another: for he that loveth another hath fulfilled the law. For this, Thou shalt not commit adultery, Thou shalt not kill, Thou shalt not steal, Thou shalt not bear false witness, Thou shalt not covet; and if there be any other commandment, it is briefly comprehended in this saying, namely, Thou shalt love thy neighbour as thyself. Love worketh no ill to his neighbour; therefore love is the fulfilling of the law.* Again in Gal. 5:14, we find: *For all the law is fulfilled in one word, even in this; Thou shalt love thy neighbour as thyself.* Jesus intimates the same truth in Matt. 22:37-40: *Jesus said unto him, Thou shalt love the Lord thy God with all thy heart, and with all thy soul, and with all thy mind. This is the first and great commandment. And the second is like unto it, Thou shalt love thy neighbour as thyself. On these two commandments hang all the law and the prophets.*

Is Sin Necessary?

Space will permit only a very brief examination of passages quoted in defense of the doctrine of sinning sainthood. Most of these are sufficiently understood when viewed in their entire context.

The phrase in the Lord's Prayer, *Forgive us our sins,* is often cited to show that there is daily sin in the believer's life. It may be sufficient to point out, as does Charles Ewing Brown in *The Meaning of Salvation,*[8] that the Lord's Prayer is a social prayer, and includes those who may have sinned. The fact, however, that our Lord immediately coupled with this phrase the condition that we forgive those who trespass against us leads one to think that our continued forgiveness for past sins is conditioned on our spirit of forgiveness toward those who sin against us. Such certainty is the teaching of the parable of the two debtors in Matt. 18:23-35.

The last part of the seventh chapter of Romans is frequently quoted as showing the certainty of sin in the Christian life. This, we saw in Chapter 1, can be maintained only by ignoring the context with its undeniable testimony to deliverance from the principle of sin and death.

Rom. 14:13, *For whatsoever is not of faith is sin*, is sometimes given to prove that any passing doubt or question in the mind is sinful. Even the most casual reading of the context will show that Paul is, in fact, arguing the ethical character of sin, and pointing out that going contrary to one's own convictions is what makes an act or practice sinful.

Jas. 4:17: *Therefore to him that knoweth to do good, and doeth it not, to him it is sin*, is supposed to indicate that falling short in any regard from the highest good known, regardless of the reason, is of the nature of sin. There is a wholesome warning against sins of omission here. Refusing to do what God commands is as much sin as doing what God forbids. However, the "therefore" prefacing the statement indicates its relationship to a context. That context warns us that we must acknowledge the will of God in all our plans. To refuse to do so is sin.

I John 1:10 is often quoted in this connection as if it read, "If we say we are not continually sinning, we make him a liar, and his word is not in us." What it actually says, of course, is, *If we say we have not sinned, we make him a liar*. No Christian denies that he at one time has sinned. It is from this sinning which he affirms himself to have been saved. All have sins to be forgiven, and unrighteousness from which to be cleansed. But there is no evidence here that he who is forgiven and cleansed must continue in sin.

John himself is the sharpest opponent of this notion in the New Testament. It is almost unbelievable that he should be quoted so often in defense of a believer's license to sin. He says, in addition to the strong passages already quoted from his first letter: *If we say that we have fellowship with him, and walk in darkness, we lie, and do not the truth* (I John 1:6). *He that saith, I know him, and keepeth not his commandments, is a liar, and the truth is not in him* (I John 2:4). *He that saith he is in the light, and hateth his brother, is in darkness even until now* (I John 2:9). *Whosoever hateth his brother is a murderer: and ye know that no murderer hath eternal life abiding in him* (I John 3:15). *We know that whosoever is born of God sinneth not; but he that is begotten of God keepeth himself, and that wicked one toucheth him not* (I John 5:18).

Lewis Sperry Chafer asserts that eradicationists, as he calls them, claim that, since their sinful nature is destroyed, they are not able to sin.[9] This would be the "sinless perfection" which Wesley staunchly disavowed, as have all holiness people since. What we affirm is not, "We are not able to sin"; but rather, "Through the regenerating and sanctifying grace of God, *we are able not to sin.*" This is scriptural, and this is the faith and experience of every victorious, sanctified child of God. *Thanks be to God, which giveth us the victory through our Lord Jesus Christ* (I Cor. 15:57).

The Nature of Christian Perfection

The bearing of this on the doctrine of Christian perfection should by now be clear. There is no such perfection as precludes the possibility of errors of judgment, mistakes in understanding, and even faults, failures, and defeats incident to any human effort. No reputable holiness teacher has ever claimed that there was such a perfection. It does not refute the Wesleyan doctrine of entire sanctification to point out such obvious imperfections. None are more conscious of them than those whose hearts are truly conformed to the mind which was in Christ Jesus.

There is no pride in evangelical perfection. That some

holiness people have given the impression of being smug and complacent is undoubtedly true. But to the degree that such an attitude has really possessed them, to that degree have they fallen short of the real implications of their profession.

On the other hand, it is quite false to state that sin is necessary in Christian life to keep the believer humble. As John Fletcher indicated in this very connection, if sin makes people humble, then Satan should possess the greatest humility. Instead, he is the prototype of all pride.

The perfection of which we speak, and which we attempt to exemplify to this lost world, is, as has been so often said, the perfection of love. *Herein is our love made perfect, that we may have boldness in the day of judgment: because as he is, so are we in this world* (I John 4:17). Such perfection cannot save from unintentional mistakes and unavoidable errors. It does lead to an immediate and humble rectifying, so far as is possible, of those faults, errors, and mistakes when they are recognized for what they are. And it does forever exclude sin in the New Testament sense: *For this is the love of God, that we keep his commandments: and his commandments are not grievous* (I John 5:3).

Chapter 4

SANCTIFICATION AND SIGNS

The fourth issue we shall consider comes from a wide-spread teaching concerning gifts of the Spirit, and their relation to Christian life as possible signs of the baptism with the Spirit. There is an important line of teaching in the New Testament relating to the gifts of the Spirit. There are numerous instances describing the exercise of these gifts. These form the scriptural background for the present-day teaching that one or more of these gifts may be considered an outward sign of the baptism with the Holy Ghost.

In our discussion of this issue, we shall rely heavily for source materials upon a book by Ralph M. Riggs entitled, *The Spirit Himself.*[1] The book has much to commend it. It is clear, temperate, and well documented. Mr. Riggs states his purpose in the Preface as follows:

> The ministers of the Pentecostal Movement have been so busy preaching the truths vouchsafed to them in these last days, that not many writers have taken time to set down in systematic form "these things which are most surely believed among us." There are now thousands of students in our Bible Institutes and Bible Colleges who must be taught, among the doctrines of Christianity, the distinctive doctrines of our Church. Our ministers likewise are in need of additional material relating to our distinctive testimony.[2]

It would seem then that one might accept this volume

as being fairly definitive of the position taken by one of the largest bodies of evangelical Christians who accept and teach the signs theory of the baptism with the Spirit. The position and purpose of its author would seem to justify this confidence.

The Baptism with the Spirit and Entire Sanctification

It is in order first to consider the relationship in the New Testament between the baptism with the Spirit and the Wesleyan doctrine of entire sanctification. These have often been separated. It has been noted that John Wesley laid little weight on the possible identity of these two operations of the divine Spirit.[3] In the present day, many who stress the importance of the baptism with (or "in" as many of them prefer) the Holy Spirit have little or nothing to say about the effect of that baptism in relation to the problem of deliverance from sin.

It is our conviction that the New Testament gives abundant warrant for assuming that the baptism with the Spirit and entire sanctification are two aspects of one and the same work of divine grace in Christian hearts. There are five points of importance here.

1. *Both Are the Heritage of Believers Only*

The baptism with the Spirit and entire sanctification are the heritage of the same class of persons, namely, those who have previously been converted. Riggs devotes two chapters[4] to this point, and rightly affirms "that, although all believers have the Holy Spirit, yet it still remains that all believers, in addition to having the Holy Spirit, may be filled with or baptized with the Holy Spirit."[5] He quotes with approval the words of R. A. Torrey, first head of the Moody Bible Institute:

It is evident that the baptism with the Holy Spirit is an operation of the Holy Spirit distinct from and addi-

tional to His regenerating work. . . . A man may be regenerated by the Holy Spirit and still not be baptized with
the Holy Spirit. In regeneration, there is the impartation
of life by the Spirit's power, and the one who receives it
is saved: in the baptism with the Holy Spirit, there is the
impartation of power, and the one who receives it is fitted
for service.[6]

Negatively, there is nowhere in the New Testament any
instance of, or promise of, any unbeliever being baptized
with or filled with the Holy Spirit. Positively, every instance
of, or promise of, any person being filled with or baptized
with the Holy Spirit is accompanied by evidence that such a
person was previously regenerated.

Similarly, the New Testament is clear on the point that
only those who have been born again can experience the
sanctifying fullness of the Holy Spirit. In His high-priestly
prayer, a prayer devoted to the great concern that God would
sanctify the disciples through His truth (John 17:17), Jesus
explicitly states, *I pray not for the world, but for them which
thou hast given me; for they are thine* (v. 9); and, *Neither
pray I for these alone, but for them also which shall believe
on me through their word* (v. 20). The Apostle Paul address-
es the Thessalonians, concerning whose status in grace
there can be little question, *And the very God of peace sanctify you wholly; and I pray God your whole spirit and soul
and body be preserved blameless unto the coming of our
Lord Jesus Christ* (I Thess. 5:23).

The basic evidence that only believers can be entirely
sanctified is found in the fact that all of the New Testament
Epistles were addressed to those identified with the Church,
and considered to be regenerated persons. Thus the score
of exhortations and admonitions to sanctification, holiness,
and purity of heart and life to be found therein are part of
the privilege and responsibility of those who have been born
again.

2. Both Are Wrought by the Spirit

Both the baptism with the Spirit and entire sanctification are accomplished by the same agency, namely, the Spirit of God. In the case of the baptism, this is shown by the very name. To be born of the Spirit is one thing; to be baptized by the Spirit is a subsequent grace. But in each case, the efficient Agent is the Third Person of the Trinity, God's Holy Spirit.

The same Spirit who regenerates likewise sanctifies. Consider, for example, I Pet. 1:2: *Elect according to the fore-knowledge of God the Father, through sanctification of the Spirit, unto obedience and sprinkling of the blood of Jesus Christ"*; or again, II Thess. 2:13: *But we are bound to give thanks alway to God for you, brethren beloved of the Lord, because God hath from the beginning chosen you to salvation through sanctification of the Spirit and belief of the truth.*

3. Both Are Given on the Same Conditions

Identical conditions are set forth in the Word for receiving both the baptism with the Spirit and entire sanctification. In a chapter on "The Baptism in the Holy Spirit, How to Receive It,"[7] Riggs sets forth four major conditions for receiving the Spirit's fullness.

First, there must be a consciousness of salvation: "We must first pray through to a know-so salvation in which the Spirit witnesses with our spirits that we are the children of God."[8]

Second, there must be obedience, involving "a perfect surrender to Him." "We are his witnesses of these things; and so is also the Holy Ghost, whom God hath given to them that obey him" (Acts 5:32).

Third, we must ask in prayer, importunately. "How much more shall your heavenly Father give the Holy Spirit to them that ask him?" (Luke 11:13)

Finally, we must believe. This is a gift, the author notes: "The Holy Spirit is a gracious, glorious, God-sent Gift, and we receive Him by faith and by faith alone. There is a 'rest of faith' into which we must enter. 'For he that is entered into his rest, he also hath ceased from his own works, as God did from his' (Hebrews 4:10)."[9]

These are exactly the conditions set forth for the experience of Christian holiness. First, there must be a consciousness that he who seeks has been born of God. Eph. 4:20-24 shows clearly that true holiness is the privilege only of those who have learned Christ, and been taught by Him.

Second, there must be consecration, a perfect surrender to the will of God. *Yield yourselves unto God, as those that are alive from the dead, and your members as instruments of righteousness unto God. . . . even so now yield your members servants to righteousness unto holiness* (Rom. 6:13, 19).

Third, there must be earnest prayer in order to enter into the grace of heart holiness. In the chapter where he stresses the "greater grace" (Jas. 4:6, ASV), and says, *Cleanse your hands, ye sinners; and purify your hearts, ye doubleminded* (v. 8), James explains spiritual shortcomings in the words, *Ye have not, because ye ask not* (v. 2).

Finally, faith must appropriate the promise of God before the believer is entirely sanctified. Jesus commissioned Paul to preach to the Gentiles, *that they may receive forgiveness of sins, and inheritance among them which are sanctified by faith that is in me* (Acts 26:18). Here, as always, *Without faith it is impossible to please him: for he that cometh to God must believe that he is, and that he is a rewarder of them that diligently seek him* (Heb. 11:6).

4. Both Accomplish the Same Results

The baptism with the Spirit and scriptural holiness are said to produce the same results. Riggs does not deal explicitly with the relation of the baptism with the Spirit to sin as a nature in the heart. He does indicate, however, that the Holy Spirit rebukes sin in the life, and states: "By Him also the believer is enabled to live a life of victory over sin. Holiness therefore is the outstanding characteristic of this member of the Trinity."[10] In his description of the meaning of the title "Spirit of Holiness" Riggs comments:

> The Spirit of Holiness, as the spirit of judgment, uncovers and condemns all that is wrong, and as the spirit of burning, purges it out. This is a work which is not so pleasant to the believer, but is very vital to the program of God. The Bride of the Lamb must be a glorious church, without spot or wrinkle or any such thing. She must be holy and without blemish. Hence the Holy Spirit is busy sanctifying and cleansing her with the washing of water by the Word. To be filled with the Holy Spirit means to allow the Holy Spirit to search out, and condemn, and destroy all the impurities of the nature and spirit.[11]

There is no doubt that the baptism with the Holy Spirit, so far as the Acts of the Apostles is concerned, resulted in the purifying of the hearts of those so baptized. Peter, in Acts 15:8-9, states that the coming of the Spirit resulted in "purifying their hearts by faith."

Likewise, entire sanctification results in the purifying or cleansing of the heart. It is said in Eph. 5:25-27, that Christ "loved the church, and gave himself" to "sanctify and cleanse it," that it might be "holy and without blemish." It should be noted that the word in the original translated "purifying" in Acts 15:9 is the same word as is translated "cleanse" in Eph. 5:26. There is given, then, in these two verses an equation of the baptism with the Holy Spirit, the sanctifying of the Church, and cleansing or purification of heart.

5. Both Have Similar Root Meanings

Both *baptism* and *sanctification* have, among other root meanings, the identical meaning of washing or cleansing from impurity. To baptize is to dip, to wash, to cleanse. To sanctify is to make holy by cleansing from all defilement.

In summary, then, the baptism with the Spirit and entire sanctification are, at most, two aspects of a work of divine grace which is one and the same. The sanctified heart is baptized with the Holy Spirit. The believer who is baptized with the Holy Spirit is entirely sanctified. The baptism with the Holy Spirit is the means whereby God effects the entire sanctification of the Christian heart. This is shown in that both are wrought upon the same class of persons; by the same agency; under the same conditions; with the same results; and even the words themselves have, among other root meanings, those that are similar.

These considerations have two very practical bearings on the Christian life. First, they disprove the teaching that the baptism with the Spirit is a "third blessing" following that of entire sanctification. There is no complete holiness without the fullness of the Holy Spirit. Second, they demonstrate that the baptism with the Holy Spirit is not only for the empowering of the Christian life; it is for the cleansing of the believer's moral nature from all depravity. The power of the Holy Spirit is the power of a clear-cut testimony backed up by a consistent life (Acts 1:8). There is power in holiness, and holiness is power (Acts 3:12).

The Evidence of the Baptism

We turn now to that part of the so-called "Pentecostal doctrine" which presents the most clear-cut challenge to the doctrine of entire sanctification as understood in the Wesleyan tradition. It is the claim that the baptism with the Spirit is evidenced always and necessarily by an initial physical sign or proof.

Riggs concedes that "a life of intimacy with God and a walk of power in the Spirit are the best proofs that one is filled with the Spirit."[12] He immediately goes on to say, however:

> The matter which is before us now is the consideration of the initial experience of receiving the Baptism and that outward physical sign which is the evidence of this experience. The Spirit-filled realm and life is so exceedingly important for the Christian that God has arranged it so that one can know very definitely whether or not he has entered into this experience. There is no mere "hope so" or need of being deceived in the matter, for God has given a physical and an audible proof of one's having received the Baptism in the Holy Spirit.[13]

That the believer can know very definitely when he has received the fullness of the Spirit, and that there is no mere "hope so" or need to be deceived in this matter, we gladly agree. The point at issue is the character of that witness, and the question whether it is always or ever "a physical and an audible proof."

Riggs considers prophecy to be the Old Testament physical and audible proof of the receiving of the Holy Spirit.[14] However, at Pentecost, he avers, the physical and audible proof became "a divine power which could enable them to speak in *other* tongues, many and varied." He says:

> On the day of Pentecost there were about fifteen different nationalities present. Among the 120 disciples who were filled with the Holy Ghost and spoke in other tongues, all fifteen languages were spoken and understood by these nationals who were present.[15]

There is something of a mystery involved in the transition which the author makes from the 15 languages spoken on the Day of Pentecost to the type of glossolalia[16] manifest in Pentecostal circles today. After describing the speaking in tongues manifest in the Book of Acts, the author concludes, "Therefore, all who receive the Baptism in the Spirit today also speak with tongues."[17]

There is on the surface of this matter a problem with

which Riggs does not deal. In the chapter following the one just quoted in which it is affirmed that the gift of tongues is the outward and audible proof of the baptism and that all who receive the baptism speak with tongues, our author gives as instances of those who received the baptism in the modern period of the Christian Church, Wesley, Gordon, Finney, and Moody. Yet there is not a shred of evidence that any of these ever spoke in an unknown tongue, either at the time of, or subsequent to, their baptism.

Until the beginning of the modern Pentecostal movement, which may be dated to the ministries of Charles F. Parham in Topeka, Kans., in 1901, and W. J. Seymour in Los Angeles in 1906-8, the only instances of unknown tongues occurred among sects which were either unorthodox or whose morality was questionable.

The Montanists, for example, were a second-century sect who practiced the speaking in unknown tongues, which they supposed found its inception in Corinth in New Testament times. However, the Montanists were branded as heretics by the Church, because they claimed a dispensation of the Spirit superior to that of Christ and the apostles.

The Port Royal Jansenists, and more particularly their successors known as the "Convulsionaries," also spoke in tongues. These were French Catholics in the early days of the Protestant Reformation. Their sect was finally suppressed by the authorities because of immoralities practiced among them.

The early spiritualists likewise spoke in unknown tongues. One, a Mary Smith of Geneva, professed to speak the language of Mars. When some of this gibberish was transcribed, scholars found it a conglomeration of sounds drawn mainly from French and German with some Oriental words mixed in.

Mary Campbell in Scotland and the followers of Edward Irving in England in the nineteenth century practiced glossolalia.

In America, the "Shakers" spoke in tongues. This was a sect founded by Ann Lee, who was known to her followers as "Mother Ann," and who made a preposterous claim to divinity by insisting on being addressed as "Ann the Word." The early Mormons, including Brigham Young, spoke in unknown tongues and their choirs sang in unknown tongues.

These facts are stated, not to prove anything concerning the present manifestation of unknown tongues among orthodox and evangelical Christians, but to show the logical problem Pentecostals must face. It is incredible that the tongue-speaking followers of the heretical sects described above should be selected as examples of those baptized with the Holy Spirit. Yet they spoke with tongues, while men like Wesley, Whitefield, Edwards, Finney, and Moody did not. If the only speaking with tongues prior to modern Pentecostalism was among heretics whose "gift" must be written off as spurious, and if tongues is the only and unfailing sign of the baptism, then it would appear by this token that none had the baptism from apostolic times through 19 centuries until modern Pentecostalism. This would be very difficult to believe.

The Gifts of the Spirit as Signs

Such considerations, while important, are not crucial. The real test of any teaching for evangelical Christians must always be its conformity to the Word of God. We turn again to scripture for light on this important question.

First, it is important that we give attention to the claim that the gifts of the Spirit are divinely intended for signs. Riggs contends that they are. Quoting Jesus, *Believe me for the very works' sake* (John 14:11); *These signs shall follow them that believe* (Mark 16:17); and Heb. 2:4, *God also bearing them witness, both with signs and wonders, and with divers miracles, and gifts of the Holy Ghost, according to his own will,* he claims, "The very fact that the gifts of the Spirit are for signs is proof that they are needed today and therefore available for us today."[18]

Again, concerning the multitudes gathered in Jerusalem on the Day of Pentecost, Riggs observes: "They overheard the disciples as they were filled with the Spirit and spoke with other tongues as the Spirit gave them utterance. On this occasion tongues were a most convincing sign to unbelievers. There have been many other occasions since when this has happened, for tongues are set 'for a sign.'"[19]

There were indeed signs and wonders done in the name of Jesus in the New Testament Church (Acts 4:30). This still does not warrant the claim that a single one of the gifts is to be regarded as proof of the baptism with the Holy Spirit. Indeed, Paul would seem to be explicitly denying the sign value of tongues so far as the Church is concerned, when he quotes Isaiah: *With men of other tongues and other lips will I speak unto this people; and yet for all that will they not hear me, saith the Lord. Wherefore tongues are for a sign, not to them that believe, but to them that believe not* (I Cor. 14:21-22). And Jesus said to those who would have a sign: *An evil and adulterous generation seeketh after a sign; and there shall no sign be given to it, but the sign of the prophet Jonas: for as Jonas was three days and three nights in the whale's belly; so shall the Son of man be three days and three nights in the heart of the earth* (Matt. 12:39-40).

Second, there is the problem as to the nature of the tongues which might conceivably be considered a sign or evidence of the baptism with the Spirit. There are, of course, two major portions of the New Testament upon which the tongues teaching is based. One is the Acts of the Apostles, notably the second chapter; and the other is I Corinthians 12 and 14. The all-important question now arises, Are these phenomena identical? Is the tongue-speaking of I Corinthians 12 and 14 the same as that of Acts 2:4? There are, naturally, two different answers which may be given to this question. Unfortunately, either answer involves rather serious difficulties for the view that unknown tongues is an evidence of the baptism with the Holy Spirit.

1. *If They Are the Same*

It may be stated that the two phenomena are the same. In that case, the tongues of the New Testament is not unknown tongues at all, but languages the speaker has not learned, but which may be recognized and understood by those who have. Mr. Riggs states[20] that no less than 15 languages were identified at the Day of Pentecost. This, I believe, is the best view that can be taken of the account in the second chapter of Acts.

The amazement of the crowds gathered in Jerusalem on that first Pentecost was not because they listened to people talking in tongues they could not understand. Their wonder was due to the fact that they heard men whom they recognized as Galileans, people notoriously provincial and illiterate, speaking with perfect diction the languages of the countries from which they had come.

As a matter of fact, the gift manifest on the Day of Pentecost, far from being unknown tongues, was given for the precise purpose of preventing the speaking in an unintelligible language. Had the apostles spoken their native Galilean dialect, their speech would have been an unknown tongue to the multitudes gathered from foreign countries. So much the rather than being unknown tongues, this gift was given to *prevent* unknown tongues.

If the answer to our question as to the relation of the

tongues of Acts 2:4 and the tongues of I Corinthians 12 and 14 be that these are the same, then two conclusions follow: (1) to speak with tongues as in Acts 2:4 is to speak a foreign language which is identifiable by those who understand that language naturally; and (2) this particular gift is expressly declared to be given to only a portion of believers, even among those who possess others of the range of spiritual gifts outlined in Corinthians. For Paul definitely states that in the body of Christ, wherein all are baptized by one Spirit (I Cor. 12:13), *not all* are prophets, apostles, teachers, workers of miracles, endowed with gifts of healing, *nor do all speak with tongues or interpret* (I Cor. 12:28-30). In the light of this passage, it is absolutely false to affirm that "all who receive the Baptism in the Spirit today also speak with tongues."[21]

2. *If They Are Different*

However, our initial question may be answered negatively. That is, it may be affirmed that the tongues of Acts 2:4 and the Corinthian tongues are not the same—that the tongues of Acts 2:4 were intelligible languages, while the tongues of Corinth were a genuine manifestation of "unknown tongues," an angelic language or utterance which can be comprehended only by those supernaturally endowed with a collateral gift of interpretation.

We are not concerned at the moment with the nature of that Corinthian gift. Not all Bible scholars are willing to concede that it was such an angelic tongue. They point out that the word "unknown" in the King James Version is printed in italics in the first Corinthian letter. This means that there was no word corresponding to it in the original, but that it was added by the translators in the hope of making the sense more intelligible. They affirm that the clause "no man understandeth" (I Cor. 14:2) may from the context be held to mean "no man present understandeth."

They state that the thrice-repeated expression "unlearned" (vv. 16, 23, and 24), in relation to those who hear but do not understand, implies that one who was "learned"—highly educated, as for instance Paul himself was—would recognize the language spoken. This is admittedly a very attractive interpretation.

Be that as it may, if the Jerusalem tongues and the Corinthian tongues were not the same, the problem for the theory that unknown tongues is an evidence of the baptism with the Spirit is just as serious. Though the tongues of I Corinthians were unknown, they still are never said to have any relation to the baptism with the Spirit. The reverse is the case. Instead of being an evidence which all Spirit-baptized believers have, the principle pertaining to gifts is directly affirmed of tongues—namely, that not all have the same gifts.

Two laws concerning the gifts of the Spirit are set forth in I Corinthians 12. The first is that the *manifestation of the Spirit is given to every man to profit withal* (v. 7). That is, gifts are given for usefulness, not as a certification of character. The second law of spiritual gifts is that different gifts are given to different people in the Church, that the body of Christ may be welded together in an indivisible unity (vv. 11-30).

The gifts of the Spirit are not in any sense a measure of the Spirit's presence within the individual believer. The disciples of Jesus before Pentecost exercised some of the more spectacular gifts. They were sent forth with authority to heal the sick and to cast out devils (Luke 9:1-6; 10:1-20), though they did not at that time experience the baptism with the Spirit. The Corinthians, whose exercise of spiritual gifts provoked the most extensive treatment given by Paul anywhere in his Epistles, were described as "carnal" and "babes in Christ" (I Cor. 3:1-3); were riven by sectarianism (3:4-7);

and were prey to all manner of irregularities in life and worship—the very antithesis of Spirit-filled believers.

The fact is indisputable that the gifts of the Spirit are quite independent of the graces of the Spirit. It is quite without scriptural warrant to claim that any of them individually or all of them collectively are designed to serve as an evidence of the baptism with the Holy Spirit.

In fact, the choice of the gift of tongues—assuming a difference between the Jerusalem tongues and the Corinthian tongues—is an extremely unfortunate one. For in each listing of the gifts, tongues and its interpretation is listed last (I Cor. 12:4-11 and 28-30); while in the list of spiritual gifts found in Rom. 12:6-8 it is omitted entirely. There is no doubt that Paul ranked the gift as decidedly inferior to the gift of prophecy, for example (I Cor. 14:1-12). His exhortations regarding gifts are to covet the best gifts (12:31), and to seek to excel in edifying the Church (14:12). And no gift, he affirms, has any value whatsoever apart from divine love (I Cor. 13:1-3), which is "a more excellent way" (12:31).

Granting a difference between the tongues of Acts 2:4 and I Corinthians 12 and 14, we should be driven to the conclusion that the only tongues which would be a possible evidence of a Pentecostal experience would be the capacity to speak a recognizable language without having learned it. Rarely has this claim been made. The tongues manifest among those who claim the evidence as in Acts 2:4 are far from what the tongues of Acts 2:4 obviously were.

But even the capacity to speak unlearned languages, impressive as it would be, would not necessarily constitute an evidence of the baptism with the Spirit. There are six occasions in the Book of Acts where groups or individuals were said to have been baptized or filled with the Spirit.[22] On three of these occasions, there was speaking in tongues. On the other three occasions, no speaking in tongues is mentioned.

An examination of the entire six instances reveals that the major point of difference between the three positive occasions and the three negative occasions is that on the positive occasions there were men of diverse nationalities together, while on the negative occasions there were men of a single nationality or race together. This would lend strong presumptive evidence to the conclusion that the purpose of the manifestation was not to serve as an evidence of the Spirit's baptism, but to make possible more effective communication within the group and to show that the gospel is for people of every language.

FAILURE OF TONGUES AS AN EVIDENCE

Any reliable evidence must be of such nature as to be present when its ground or occasion is present, and to be absent when its ground or occasion is absent. Dr. B. F. Neely many years ago showed that such is not the case in the relationship between tongues and the baptism of the Holy Ghost.

Pentecostal people readily admit that the gift may be "counterfeited," that Satan may impart tongues as well as the Spirit of God. The presence of the phenomenon among the false sects mentioned earlier indicates that this is unquestionably true. It is possible for those who have never had the baptism with the Holy Spirit to speak with tongues.

Again, Pentecostal people readily admit that gifts may be retained by one who has, through sin, forfeited the presence of the Holy Spirit. One who has the gift of tongues may continue to exercise this gift long after the Spirit has departed from him. It is thus possible for those who have lost the baptism with the Holy Spirit to speak with tongues.

This then results in a curious situation. When a person speaks with tongues, it is an evidence of one of three things: first, he has the baptism with the Holy Spirit; second, he has had the baptism and has lost it; or third, he has never had the baptism. But obviously these three statements take in every living human being. It can be said that wearing a hat is as reliable an evidence of the baptism with the Holy Spirit as is the gift of tongues. For everyone who wears a hat has the baptism, has had it and lost it, or has never had it. The evidential value of any such gift is therefore precisely nil.

THE WITNESS OF THE SPIRIT

What then? Are we reduced to a state of uncertainty concerning this high state of grace? Indeed we are not. There is an evidence of the baptism with the Holy Spirit—and entire sanctification, which is its result and concomitant—which surpasses in certainty any possible outward physical sign. It is the twofold evidence of the witness of the Spirit and the fruit of the Spirit.

Just as *he that believeth on the Son of God hath the witness in himself* (I John 5:10), so he who receives the Spirit of God in His fullness has the witness to that wonderful gift of God's grace, for *it is the Spirit that beareth witness, because the Spirit is truth* (I John 5:6). Just as the Holy Spirit bears witness to the heart of the believer that he is God's child (Rom. 8:14-17), so *by one offering he hath perfected for ever them that are sanctified. Whereof the Holy Ghost also is a witness to us* (Heb. 10:14-15). This witness is certified by the divine law written in the heart and mind, giving *boldness to enter into the holiest by the blood of Jesus,* so that we may *draw near with a true heart in full assurance of faith, having our hearts sprinkled from an evil conscience, and our bodies washed with pure water* (vv. 16, 19, and 22).

This witness is not an emotion, an exhilaration, an ecstasy of joy, although it may result in such feelings. It is not an outward manifestation or demonstration. It is the inward conviction that what God has promised, that He has performed; that the work of cleansing has been completed; and that the Holy Spirit abides in all the glories of His sanctifying lordship. *When the Comforter is come,* said Jesus, *whom I will send unto you from the Father, even the Spirit of truth, which proceedeth from the Father, he shall testify of me. . . . he will guide you into all truth . . . He shall glorify me: for he shall receive of mine, and shall shew it unto you* (John 15:26; 16:13-14).

Coupled with the witness of the Spirit, as John Wesley insisted long ago, must be the fruit of the Spirit. These nine beautiful graces—love, joy, peace, long-suffering, gentleness, goodness, faith, meekness, and temperance (Gal. 5:22) —are subject to almost limitless growth and development, but all are present as features of the Spirit-filled personality. Neither the witness without the fruit nor the fruit without the witness can be accepted as complete evidence. Both together, they provide a degree of certitude far beyond anything offered by external physical or psychological signs.

As one need not go forth in the morning with lighted candle to see if the sun has risen, no more need the sanctified heart depend upon some fallible manifestation to know that the "Sun of righteousness" has arisen in his heart with healing for sin's cancerous nature within. The Spirit himself bears witness to His abiding fullness within.

Chapter 5

SANCTIFICATION AND SECURITY

The need for security is one of the most pressing and imperative of human needs. Feelings of insecurity have been found to lie back of the most serious misconduct on the part of children and young people. Nothing is more fatal to happiness than uncertainty and the lack of some degree of security for the future.

This principle holds with regard to the spiritual life. To be plagued by doubts, questionings, and fears is to be defeated before the battle starts. Confidence and reasonable hopes are essential ingredients for a happy Christian life. If salvation cannot supply the need for security, it falls short by so much of meeting the whole range of human needs.

One of the sharpest issues in modern-day evangelical circles centers about this admitted need. It arises from the position taken by a large and influential group of pastors, evangelists, radio preachers, churches, and institutions to the effect that a single act of saving faith in an initial acceptance of Christ insures the final and eternal salvation of the believer.

In some cases, this position is based on the Calvinistic doctrine of particular election. This is the claim that God has from all eternity chosen some men and angels to eternal life, and has left all others to eternal damnation. No one has ever stated it more succinctly than John Calvin himself.

> Predestination we call the eternal decree of God by which He hath determined in Himself what He would have to become of every individual of mankind. For they are not all created with a similar destiny; but eternal life is foreordained for some, and eternal damnation for others. . . . We assert that, by an eternal and immutable counsel, God hath once for all determined whom He would admit to salvation and whom He would condemn to destruction. We affirm that this counsel, as far as concerns the elect, is founded on His gratuitous mercy, totally irrespective of human merit: but that to those whom He devotes to condemnation, the gate of life is closed by a just and irreprehensible, but incomprehensible judgment.[1]

Lewis Sperry Chafer quotes Cunningham's *Historical Theology* with approval: "If it be true God has, from eternity, absolutely and unconditionally chosen some men certain persons, to eternal life, these men assuredly will all infallibly be saved."[2]

The formal truth of this proposition must be admitted. If salvation is by the unconditional predestination of the elect to eternal life, then unquestionably all so predestinated will be finally saved. But the consequent "These men assuredly will all infallibly be saved" obviously hangs entirely upon the material truth of its antecedent, "If God has unconditionally chosen some to eternal life."

We have not space here to debate the dogma of unconditional predestination. It has been refuted by able theologians and stands in opposition to a score or more of definite biblical promises of salvation to any and all who meet God's terms.[3] We want only to point out that this doctrine of predestination, instead of establishing certainty of final salvation in the individual believer's mind, actually destroys it.

It is true that, under this view, if one is predestined to be saved, he will be saved, no matter what he may do or fail to do. It is also true that if salvation is by the eternal, immutable, and incomprehensible decree of God without conditions applying to the individual, no one has the right to conclude infallibly that he is in that elect group, however religious he may feel.

This turns out to be a curious sort of security. In effect one says, "If I am elected to eternal life, I am eternally secure. But I cannot, in the nature of the case, be sure that I am so elected. I can but hope, humbled by the remembrance of multitudes who, though they were with us, yet *went out from us*, for they *were not of us: for if they had been of us, they would no doubt have continued with us: but they went out, that they might be made manifest that they were not all of us*" (I John 2:19—a favorite Calvinistic text).

The Neo-Calvinistic Concept of Security

In the majority of cases, however, the doctrine of eternal security is not grounded on the Calvinistic dogma of unconditional predestination. While all who teach eternal security are frequently called "Calvinists," actually the greater portion of them are no more than 20 percent Calvinistic. That is, they hold no more than one out of the famous "five points" of the Calvinistic-Arminian debate.[4] These 80 percent Arminians should not be called Calvinists at all, strictly speaking—but the usage has become so widespread it doubtless will continue. "Neo-Calvinism" would be a more accurate classification.

What is widely hailed as the best and most complete presentation of this modern form of the doctrine of eternal security is presented in a book written by a layman, Mr. J. H. Strombeck, entitled *Shall Never Perish*.[5] Since this seems to be regarded as authoritative, it will be largely the basis of our presentation of the position, and criticisms of it. In the main, the book is a serious effort to establish the doctrine of eternal security on biblical evidence.

It should be stated at the outset that it is not the concept of the security of God's obedient children which is disturbing. We quite agree that all Christ's sheep are safe, that no one can pluck them out of the Father's hand, that no creature can separate the believer from the love of God which is in Christ Jesus, our Lord. That is all blessedly true.

As has been said, it is not the doctrine of the perseverance of the saints that disturbs us, but the doctrine of the perseverance of sinners. It is the underlying assumption, which becomes explicit all too often, that a single act of saving faith initially ends all probation, and insures the final salvation of the individual regardless of any future faith or lack of it, and without respect to sinfulness or righteousness of life. Mr. Strombeck strongly disavows antinomianism—that is, the idea that the Christian is free from all obligation to the moral law—yet even he sometimes directly affirms it, and it is the natural outcome of every page he writes.

To take this book page by page, as a thorough consideration would demand and as the book well deserves, would be impossible in the space available here. We can but express some of the major points and make brief comments thereon.

The title chapter of the book, "Shall Never Perish," is an exposition of John 10:27-29, "My sheep hear my voice, and I know them, and they follow me: and I give unto them eternal life; and they shall never perish, and no one shall snatch them out of my hand. My Father, who hath given them unto me, is greater than all; and no one is able to snatch them out of the Father's hand" (ASV).

Strombeck comments:

> For the believer in the Lord Jesus Christ, no passage in the Bible has more assurance in it than has this one. In it is found an unconditional statement by our Lord that those who are His are His for all eternity, because they are in His hand, under His care, and are in the Father's hand, under His care. The strength of the Father is that which guarantees this condition of safety.[6]

We quite agree that this passage makes the unconditional assertion, "No one of Christ's sheep shall be lost." There are no ifs, ands, or buts about it. But it must also be pointed out that it makes just as unconditional an assertion that all Christ's sheep hear His voice and follow Him, and no person who does not hear His voice and follow Him is one of His sheep. This does not add an "if" where God has not put one. It merely points out what Jesus stated as plainly as words can put it: He who does not follow is not of Christ's flock.

Reduced to its simplest logic, this passage states:

All who are secure are Christ's sheep;

None who do not follow are His sheep;

Therefore, none who do not follow are secure.

Mr. Strombeck strongly believes (Chapters 2, 5—7) that the doctrines of grace are incomplete without the conclusion expressed in the doctrine of eternal security. Since salvation is by grace, its continuance cannot be by meritorious works. With this we quite agree. We would only point out that salvation is by grace through faith no less when its *retention* is regarded as conditional than when its *reception* is regarded as conditional. If the faith which *retains* salvation constitutes "meritorious works," then so does the faith which *receives* salvation. But faith is never a meritorious act.[7] Grace is no less grace because faith retains it than it is grace because faith receives it. A gift is no less a gift when it should be prized highly and guarded jealously than when it may be treated as inviolate whether prized or not.

In Chapter 3 of Strombeck's book, we are assured that whether one is saved or lost is not determined by his manner of life, but by what God says. We certainly agree that what God says is the important thing. Furthermore, God has spoken in no uncertain terms on this point. But He has not said that it makes no difference to salvation how one lives. For instance:

Matt. 7:16-21: *Ye shall know them by their fruits. Do men gather grapes of thorns, or figs of thistles? Even so every good tree bringeth forth good fruit; but a corrupt tree bringeth forth evil fruit. A good tree cannot bring forth evil fruit, neither can a corrupt tree bring forth good fruit. Every tree that bringeth not forth good fruit is hewn down, and cast into the fire. Wherefore by their fruits ye shall know them. Not every one that saith unto me, Lord, Lord, shall enter into the kingdom of heaven; but he that doeth the will of my Father which is in heaven.*

Does this read as if one's manner of life makes no difference in salvation?

Consider the following passages of scripture:

Rom. 6:1, 15: *What shall we say then? Shall we continue in sin, that grace may abound? What then? shall we sin, because we are not under the law, but under grace? God forbid.* Does this read as if one's manner of life makes no difference in salvation?

I Cor. 3:16-17: *Know ye not that ye are the temple of God, and that the Spirit of God dwelleth in you? If any man defile the temple of God, him shall God destroy; for the temple of God is holy, which temple ye are.* Does this sound as if one's manner of life makes no difference in salvation?

Gal. 2:17-18: *But if, while we seek to be justified by Christ, we ourselves also are found sinners, is therefore*

Christ the minister of sin? God forbid. For if I build again the things which I destroyed, I make myself a transgressor. Does this sound as if one's manner of life makes no difference in salvation?

Rom. 8:14: *For as many as are led by the Spirit of God, they are the sons of God.* Does this sound as if one's manner of life makes no difference in salvation?

Jas. 2:17: *Even so faith, if it hath not works, is dead, being alone.* I John 3:10: *In this the children of God are manifest, and the children of the devil: whosoever doeth not righteousness is not of God, neither he that loveth not his brother.* Does this sound as if one's manner of life makes no difference in salvation?

God *has* spoken. God has declared in His eternal Word that, while one's manner of life does not *purchase* salvation, it does *prove* it. He who lives in sin is a sinner, whatever he may call himself, and whatever he may have been in the past.

In Chapter 4, Strombeck gives us a splendid collation of verses regarding eternal life and final salvation. Each one means exactly what it says. But these scriptures are unfairly interpreted by the neo-Calvinists to mean *more* than they say in order to support their theory that a single act of faith guarantees final salvation.

Eternal Security and Antinomianism

It is in Part II of the book that the nose of the antinomian camel begins to appear in the eternal security tent. This is a section on "Eternal Security and Some Doctrines of the Grace of God." Here we read that all individual verses which might seem to discredit the doctrine of eternal security must be interpreted in harmony with what the author happily calls "grace truth."[8] Thus, it really *isn't* what God says that is to be taken at face value, but how these words may be interpreted in harmony with a preconceived concept of "grace."

Since salvation is by grace and not by works, Strombeck says, "Therefore demerit [that is, sin] does not hinder the operation of grace, nor can it set aside that which grace has accomplished. In fact, demerit [or sin] is the occasion for grace to accomplish its work."[9] How much this is like the theory Paul disclaims with such vigor in Romans 6:1-2: *Shall we continue in sin, that grace may abound? God forbid.*

On page 28, printed in italics, Strombeck makes his meaning unmistakably clear: *"If every possible vestige of human merit is excluded* [by the fact that salvation is by grace through faith], *then man's acts, apart from accepting the Savior, are not related to salvation and thus no act of man or demerit of man can cause him to be taken out of the condition of being saved."*

That Strombeck means what he seems to say is further evidenced by a statement on page 131 wherein the author lists examples of these "acts of demerit" which cannot affect the believer's salvation, and includes everything from "hasty unkind words" to "theft, falsification [lying], idolatry, drunkenness, revellings, fornication, adultery, murder." None of these sins can affect the believer's condition of being saved, we are told. "As far as the penalty of God's holy law and the demands of His righteousness are concerned, the sin question is settled once and for all the very moment an individual believes that Christ paid the penalty in his place."[10]

It is hard to maintain moderation when dealing with extreme views such as this. Let it be said, this is not grace; this is disgrace.

Strombeck is not alone in this antinomianism. It plagues the theory of eternal security wherever it appears For example, Evangelist John R. Rice writes:

So, though a Christian may lose sweet fellowship with the Father by his sins, yet he is still God's child, partaker of the divine nature. God punishes His children when they sin, but they are His children still.[11]

One of the most fearless statements of the antinomianism which is latent in this view of "grace" is found in the book by August Van Ryn, *The Epistles of John.* In the comment on I John 5:16, "There is a sin unto death," he says:

The Apostle probably is referring to sin in a believer's life so serious that God cannot permit such an one to continue to live on earth. It has been said that a believer is fit to go to heaven, yet may not be fit to live on earth. . . . This may mean for such to be taken away by death, because they so dishonor the name of Christ that they can no longer be permitted to remain on earth. They are redeemed by the blood of Christ and thus fit to go to heaven, but their lives are so displeasing to God that they cannot be allowed to remain on earth.[12]

This carries the position of eternal security to its logical outcome, and as such it is almost self-refuting. How utterly contrary this is to the Word of God! The evidence of Scripture has been considered in part, at least, in Chapter 3 of this study, and will be further shown in the section following.

Coming back to Strombeck's statement that "men's acts, apart from accepting the Savior, are not related to salvation," one wonders why, if "accepting the Savior" is related to salvation, rejecting the Saviour is not also vitally related. Indeed, Heb. 6:4-6 definitely asserts that it does affect salvation: *For it is impossible for those who were once enlightened, and have tasted of the heavenly gift, and were made partakers of the Holy Ghost, and have tasted the good word of God, and the powers of the world to come, if they shall fall away, to renew them again unto repentance; seeing they crucify to themselves the Son of God afresh, and put him to an open shame.* If this does not say that final apostasy is possible, then language means nothing at all.

To say that no sin can affect a believer's final salvation is to fly right in the face of God's Word. Isa. 59:1-2 reads: *Behold, the Lord's hand is not shortened, that it cannot save; neither his ear heavy, that it cannot hear; but your iniquities have separated between you and your God, and your sins have hid his face from you, that he will not hear.*

No person, no power, no *thing* can separate a soul from God. But sin is not a person, power, or thing. It is a choice, an act of the will, an attitude of the soul. Sin can and will always separate the sinning soul from the presence of God.

Let us consider three other passages in this connection:

Ezek. 33:12: *Therefore, thou son of man, say unto the children of thy people, The righteousness of the righteous shall not deliver him in the day of his transgression . . . neither shall the righteous be able to live for his righteousness in the day that he sinneth.*

Rev. 21:8: *But the fearful, and unbelieving, and the abominable, and murderers, and whoremongers, and sorcerers, and idolaters, and all liars, shall have their part in the lake which burneth with fire and brimstone: which is the second death.*

Rev. 22:19: *And if any man shall take away from the words of the book of this prophecy, God shall take away his part out of the book of life, and out of the holy city, and from the things which are written in this book.*

Does any of this sound as if "men's acts, apart from accepting the Savior, are not related to salvation"? Where is there anywhere in the Bible warrant for the notion that "a believer is fit to go to heaven" who "may not be fit to live on earth"? Of what value are the dogmas of men—even men who are personally devout—if they make license for sin in Christian life, and deny the Word of God? *He that saith, I know him, and keepeth not his commandments, is a liar, and the truth is not in him* (I John 2:4).

The doctrines of grace are precious to the believer's

heart, but they cannot be made a cloak for sin.* Salvation is by grace only, never by works. But salvation is *no less of grace* by reason of being a present-tense relationship with God, maintained, as it was obtained, by a living and vital faith.

The obedience of faith is in no sense a meritorious work. If it be by grace through faith, then it is not of works. Let us remember that *the grace of God that bringeth salvation hath appeared to all men, teaching us that, denying ungodliness and worldly lusts, we should live soberly, righteously, and godly, in this present world* (Titus 2:11-12). It does not teach us that nothing a believer ever can do will affect his final salvation.

What Saith the Lord?

But enough for the logical approach to this problem. Our author complains that those who oppose the doctrine of eternal security never quote scripture, but simply make unfounded statements. Having in mind the eternal security claim, let us see what "saith the Lord."

We shall arrange our collations of scripture in two major groups: those passages which teach that final salvation rests on continued faith as well as initial faith; and those which make direct assertion of the possibility of the final apostasy of regenerated persons. Out of a total of more than 80 passages, some selection is obviously necessary, and only a few from each group will be noted here. To these must be added the verses quoted earlier in this chapter and in Chapter 3 which indicate that no child of God lives in sin.

1. *The Nature of Saving Faith*

Final salvation is by grace through a faith which is not a single act but a constant attitude resulting in an obedient walk. Dr. Daniel Steele, in the excerpt from *Milestone*

Papers quoted at the close of Chapter 2, has carefully examined all New Testament references to faith in relation to final or eternal salvation. In each case, the present tense is used, indicating the continuing character of faith. It cannot be argued that if one is once a believer he is therefore always a believer. I once believed in Santa Claus, but no more. Faith, to be effective, must be continuous.

But apart from the meaning of the tenses, the voice of Scripture is clear. We are chided by Strombeck for putting an "if" where there is none.[13] What can we say for those who take the "if" away from the places where God has put it? Think how we would have to read the following passages, for example, should the current doctrine of eternal security be true.

John 8:31 says: *Then said Jesus to those Jews which believed on him, If ye continue in my word, then are ye my disciples indeed.* This would have to be changed to read, "Whether or not ye continue in My word, ye are My disciples indeed."

John 8:51 reads, *Verily, verily, I say unto you, If a man keep my saying, he shall never see death.* We must correct our Lord's misstatement if we are to harmonize with the teaching of eternal security, and read, "Even he that does not continue in My word, if he was ever saved, shall never see death."

Paul, in Col. 1:22-23, made a very grave error, according to our eternal security friends, when he spoke of Christ's purpose *to present you holy and unblameable and unreproveable in his sight: if ye continue in the faith grounded and settled, and be not moved away from the hope of the gospel.*

The Epistle to the Hebrews, in chapter 3, verse 6, would be in error in saying Christ is a *son over his own house; whose house are we, if we hold fast the confidence and the rejoicing of the hope firm unto the end.* He should rather have said, "Whose house are we, even if we do not hold fast our hope."

Peter, and even John, fail to rightly represent the believer's eternal and unconditional security. Peter says, *Wherefore the rather, brethren, give diligence to make your calling and election sure: for if ye do these things, ye shall never fall* (II Pet. 1:10). John exhorts, *Let that therefore abide in you, which ye have heard from the beginning. If that which ye have heard from the beginning shall remain in you, ye also shall continue in the Son, and in the Father* (I John 2:24). Peter should have said, "Wherefore the rather, brethren, recognize that your calling and election is already sure: whatever ye do, ye shall never fall." John ought to have written, "There are no ifs or questions about it; ye shall continue in the Son and in the Father."

The teaching of God's Word is unmistakable. These are all conditional propositions. In a conditional proposition, the portion containing the condition is known as the antecedent; the portion expressing the conclusion is known as the consequent. The most elementary textbook in logic will state that *the consequent of a conditional statement can be affirmed only when the antecedent is first affirmed.*

Our eternal security friends teach that a single, historical act of faith forever establishes the believer's standing with God. Even subsequent unbelief, which is a form of sin, cannot imperil final salvation, Strombeck explicitly avers.[14]

This is definitely contradicted in the Bible. For instance, Paul writes to the Corinthians: *Moreover, brethren, I declare unto you the gospel which I preached unto you, which also ye have received, and wherein ye stand; by which also ye are saved, if ye keep in memory what I preached unto you, unless ye have believed in vain* (I Cor. 15:1-2). Here is another conditional statement: *By which ye are saved, if ye keep in memory what I preached unto you.* This is a direct assertion that their first faith might be in vain, not by reason of any unfaithfulness on the part of God, but by reason of their own negligence in keeping the gospel.

Again in II Cor. 1:24, Paul says, *Not for that we have dominion over your faith, but are helpers of your joy: for by faith ye stand.* "By faith ye stand"—there is no standing apart from that continuing faith.

In I Tim. 6:12, Paul admonishes, *Fight the good fight of faith, lay hold on eternal life, whereunto thou art also called, and hast professed a good profession before many witnesses.* Either young Timothy was not yet born again— which is incredible—or the fact of a new birth does not alone and of itself seal final salvation, as the eternal security advocates claim.

In Heb. 3:12-14, the apostle speaks to his brethren in Christ in terms that are utterly meaningless if this doctrine be true: *Take heed, brethren, lest there be in any of you an evil heart of unbelief, in departing from the living God. But exhort one another daily, while it is called To day; lest any of you be hardened through the deceitfulness of sin. For we are made partakers of Christ, if we hold fast the beginning of our confidence stedfast unto the end.* This certainly does not sound as if one single initial act of faith forever secures salvation. There is a continuance in faith which is just as necessary as the first believing.

Peter shares the same opinion, for in I Pet. 1:5 he says, *Who are kept by the power of God through faith unto salvation ready to be revealed in the last time.* We are kept, not independent of our faith, but *through faith.* And we are kept through faith unto a final salvation which is not an inalienable possession now but which is "ready to be revealed in the last time."

It is hard to know where to draw the line in this citation of scripture evidence that the believer's salvation is a present-tense walk with God. It is hard to omit Rom. 2:6-7, *Who will render to every man according to his deeds: to*

85

them who by patient continuance in well doing seek for glory and honour and immortality, eternal life. It is difficult to skip Heb. 5:9, *And being made perfect, he became the author of eternal salvation unto all them that obey him.* One can hardly ignore Rev. 3:5, *He that overcometh, the same shall be clothed in white raiment; and I will not blot out his name out of the book of life, but I will confess his name before my Father, and before his angels.*

For, if the doctrine of eternal security be true, then all these verses, and a dozen others which might be added, are entirely without meaning, if not utterly false. But we say, "Let God be true," and if necessary, "every man a liar." No doctrine can be acceptable which renders false or meaningless so much of the Word of God.

2. The Possibility of Final Apostasy

In addition to those references which indicate a continuing as well as a historical faith as the condition for final salvation, there are a great number[15] which definitely assert the possibility of the final apostasy of those who at some past time have savingly believed. A sampling includes the following:

Matt. 18:34-35: *And his lord was wroth, and delivered him to the tormentors, till he should pay all that was due unto him. So likewise shall my heavenly Father do also unto you, if ye from your hearts forgive not every one his brother their trespasses.* The context makes it crystal-clear that those who were forgiven will again answer for their sins if they, in their turn, refuse to forgive those who sin against them.

Luke 8:13: *They on the rock are they, which, when they hear, receive the word with joy; and these have no root, which for a while believe, and in time of temptation fall away.* This is a parable—but a parable teaches truth. Here the truth is that there are some believers, who receive the Word with joy, who later fall away and perish.

Luke 12:42-46: *And the Lord said, Who then is that faithful and wise steward, whom his lord shall make ruler over his household, to give them their portion of meat in due season? Blessed is that servant, whom his lord when he cometh shall find so doing. Of a truth I say unto you, that he will make him ruler over all that he hath. But and if that servant say in his heart, My lord delayeth his coming; and shall begin to beat the menservants and maidens, and to eat and drink, and to be drunken; the lord of that servant will come in a day when he looketh not for him, and at an hour when he is not aware, and will cut him in sunder, and will appoint him his portion with the unbelievers.* It will not do to say that Jesus here was talking about servants and not sons or friends,[16] unless one is willing to grant that a servant and not a son or friend may be ruler over all that He has. It is obviously the same servant—in one case faithful and wise, in the other untrue and faithless.

Rom. 11:20-22: *Well; because of unbelief they were broken off, and thou standest by faith. Be not highminded, but fear: for if God spared not the natural branches, take heed lest he also spare not thee. Behold therefore the goodness and severity of God: on them which fell, severity; but toward thee, goodness, if thou continue in his goodness: otherwise thou also shalt be cut off.* Continuance in God's goodness is necessary to final salvation.

I Cor. 8:10-11: *For if any man see thee which hast knowledge sit at meat in the idol's temple, shall not the conscience of him which is weak be emboldened to eat those things which are offered to idols; and through thy knowledge shall the weak brother perish, for whom Christ died?* A testimony to the importance of influence, these verses are also a witness to the fact that brethren for whom Christ died *may* perish if the influence of stronger Christians is not what it ought to be.

Gal. 5:1, 4: *Stand fast therefore in the liberty where-*

with Christ hath made us free, and be not entangled again with the yoke of bondage. Christ is become of no effect unto you, whosoever of you are justified by the law; ye are fallen from grace. These words were spoken to young Christians being tempted to give up their faith in Christ to return to the law. They are plainly told that so to do is to fall from grace.

I Thess. 3:5: *For this cause, when I could no longer forbear, I sent to know your faith, lest by some means the tempter have tempted you, and our labour be in vain.* If the Thessalonians were eternally secure, how could the apostle have concern lest his labor should be in vain?

I Tim. 4:1: *Now the Spirit speaketh expressly, that in the latter times some shall depart from the faith, giving heed to seducing spirits, and doctrines of devils.* One cannot depart from what one has never possessed. The last days are times of apostasy.

Heb. 10:26-29: *For if we sin wilfully after that we have received the knowledge of the truth, there remaineth no more sacrifice for sins, but a certain fearful looking for of judgment and fiery indignation, which shall devour the adversaries. He that despised Moses' law died without mercy under two or three witnesses; of how much sorer punishment, suppose ye, shall he be thought worthy, who hath trodden under foot the Son of God, and hath counted the blood of the covenant, wherewith he was sanctified, an unholy thing, and hath done despite unto the Spirit of grace?* This is a strong declaration of the possibility of final apostasy, even on the part of those who were sanctified by the Blood of the covenant. It leaves no open question.

Jas. 5:19-20: *Brethren, if any of you do err from the truth, and one convert him; let him know that he which converteth the sinner from the error of his way shall save a soul from death, and shall hide a multitude of sins.* This is clearly spoken of those commonly known as backsliders—who were brethren, but have erred from the truth. If such are converted, a soul is saved from death, and a multitude of sins hidden beneath the precious Blood.

II Pet. 2:20-21: *For if after they have escaped the pollutions of the world through the knowledge of the Lord and Saviour Jesus Christ, they are again entangled therein, and overcome, the latter end is worse with them than the beginning. For it had been better for them not to have known the way of righteousness, than, after they have known it, to turn from the holy commandment delivered unto them.* It is useless to explain this away as human reformation. The whole letter is a ringing warning to the Church to beware of the influence of false prophets, destroying the faith and damning the souls of those who have believed. These words could never be spoken unless the possibility of final apostasy were real indeed.

II John 8-9: *Look to yourselves, that we lose not those things which we have wrought, but that we receive a full reward. Whosoever transgresseth, and abideth not in the doctrine of Christ, hath not God. He that abideth in the doctrine of Christ, he hath both the Father and the Son.* Abiding in the doctrine and avoiding transgression—these are perpetual conditions for the possession of God and hope of eternal life.

Thus saith the Lord.

SECURITY: TRUE AND FALSE

The security we enjoy in Christ does not mean the absence of danger. A false security, denying the existence of danger, is the worst possible state of mind. Real security can exist only when there is an awareness of possible peril, and of the availability of resources to meet it. It is he who "thinketh he standeth" who is in real danger of falling (I Cor. 10:12).

There is a strange paradox here. Both sanctification and

security have two sides—a divine side and a human side. Our neo-Calvinistic friends deny the divine side to sanctification, considering it for all practical purposes to be but human consecration. On the other hand, they deny the human side of security, and make it all to depend upon the divine. The remedy for both errors is to recognize the true nature of divine grace: a divine enabling freely made available to all who will; a partnership with God for both the salvation of the soul and the redemption of a lost race.

There *is* real security for every believer in Christ. It is not in some fantastic misreading of the doctrines of grace, but in a living relationship with God. Some of our eternal security brethren have a strange notion as to what we teach. They talk about "the Arminian doctrine of insecurity" (Chafer) and the believer's "loss of assurance" (Strombeck). In an article on "Security of the Believer," Douglas C. Hartley writes:

> The Christian who holds that he can be lost loses much, and being of "a doubtful mind" (Luke 12:29) cannot serve God as he ought. Truly, many such exceed in service some who embrace security, but having to be concerned about themselves, their service cannot rise to full capacity. Neither can they experience fully the joy of salvation; freedom from fear of death while lost; knowledge that Christ fully satisfies; nor, because of concern for themselves, can they share fully God's own concern for the unsaved.
>
> How, too, can they recommend to others One whom they cannot fully trust? Their own faith is lacking because they will not—cannot—trust themselves completely to the love of God as expressed in the finished work of Christ, nor to the promises and privileges of either. They must rely on their own weak strength, instead of the power of the Almighty, to "walk as children of light" (Eph. 5:8). Being slaves to fear because, to them, Christ's sacrifice has not freed them fully from the law, they have not "been called unto liberty" (Gal. 5:13). They will not believe that "the truth shall make you free" (John 8:32). [17]

This is a complete misrepresentation of the Arminian-Wesleyan position. As a matter of fact, in the history of Protestantism the doctrine of Christian assurance is directly the contribution of the Wesleyan revival. The writer has yet to meet his first Arminian Christian brother who was plagued with this imaginary sense of being in peril of the loss of his soul.

The born-again child of God no more fears being lost than he fears that he may commit suicide physically. He does not have to be told that he cannot possibly commit suicide in order to be delivered from fear of death at his own hand. The only possible basis for lack of Christian assurance is condemnation for sin. For such condemnation, God has provided an instant and complete remedy, as noted in Chapter 3. For one who becomes despondent through fear of backsliding, there are a hundred who are led into the morass of antinomian carelessness by the doctrine of unconditional security.

The security of the Christian soul lies in the present-tense character of the grace of God: grace that saves; grace that sanctifies; and grace that keeps.

This is security without presumption.

It is safety for the soul without license to sin.

It reaches its apex in the entire sanctification of the believer's heart, destroying the inner propensity to sin, and perfecting the love of God within. *Therefore being justified by faith, we have peace with God through our Lord Jesus Christ: by whom also we have access by faith into this grace wherein we stand, and rejoice in hope of the glory of God* (Rom. 5:1-2). *Follow peace with all men, and holiness, without which no man shall see the Lord: looking diligently lest any man fail of* (margin, "fall from") *the grace of God, lest any root of bitterness springing up trouble you, and thereby many be defiled* (Heb. 12:14-15).

In the presence of the Holy Spirit in the believer's heart,

91

there is *internal* security. His is the blessed work of guiding into all truth, securing the soul against overwhelming temptation, and providing grace which makes us "more than conquerors through him that loved us" (Rom. 8:37).

Reference Notes

CHAPTER 1

1. Lewis Sperry Chafer, *Systematic Theology* (Dallas, Tex.: Dallas Seminary Press, 1947), VI, 270.

2. There is a ceremonial holiness which pertains to things and days, which is occasionally applied to persons, even unbelievers (cf. I Cor. 7:14). This, however, is never represented in the Bible as the acme of holiness for the believer, as is positional holiness. For an excellent treatment of ceremonial holiness, see Charles Ewing Brown, *The Meaning of Sanctification* (Anderson, Ind.: The Warner Press, 1945), pp. 138-43.

3. Cf. the counterpart of these verses in Col. 3:5-10.

4. *Op. cit.*, VI, 288.

CHAPTER 2

1. *Ibid.*, VI, 284-85.

2. See Chapter 4 for evidence identifying the baptism with the Holy Spirit and entire sanctification.

3. Cf. Chapter 4.

4. The climaxing fullness of the Spirit was accepted by the Jerusalem church as convincing evidence that Gentiles were also "granted repentance unto life" (Acts 11:18). "Saved" as in Acts 11:14 is not a synonym of "converted," but includes God's total redemptive work in the heart.

5. Dwight L. Moody, *Secret Power* (Chicago: The Bible Institute Colportage Association, 1908), pp. 16, 50.

6. Daniel Steele, *Milestone Papers* (New York: Eaton and Mains, 1878), "The Tense Readings of the Greek New Testament," pp. 53-90. This has recently been reprinted in an appendix to Charles Ewing Brown, *The Meaning of Sanctification.* A more complete summation has been made by Drs. Olive M. Winchester and Ross E. Price in their book, *Crisis Experiences in the Greek New Testament* (Kansas City: Beacon Hill Press, 1953).

7. William Hersey Davis, *Beginner's Grammar of the Greek*

New Testament (New York: George Doran Co., 1923), p. 123 (italics in original).

8. Hadley, *Greek Grammar for Schools and Colleges*, quoted by Winchester and Price, *op. cit.*

9. Quoted by Winchester and Price, *ibid.*

10. *Op. cit.*, pp. 57, 59, 65-66.

11. *Ibid.*, p. 90.

Chapter 3

1. (Kansas City: Beacon Hill Press, 1945).

2. *Op. cit.*, VI, 185.

3. (Kansas City: Beacon Hill Press of Kansas City, 1966), pp. 53-54.

4. The same method, obviously, may be used to determine the meaning of the noun forms of the word "sin," and all other New Testament related forms. Inasmuch as there are some 300 such uses in the the New Testament alone, this is too large a task to be undertaken here.

5. The list, taken from Young's *Analytical Concordance*, is as follows: Acts 25:8; Matt. 18:15; Luke 17:3-4; I Pet. 2:20; Matt. 18:21; 27:4; Luke 15:18, 21; John 5:14; 8:11; 9:2-3; Rom. 2:12; 3:23; 5:12, 14, 16; 6:15; I Cor. 6:18; 7:28, 36; 8:12; 15:34; Eph. 4:26; I Tim. 5:20; Titus 3:11; Heb. 3:17; 10:26; II Pet. 2:4; I John 1:10; 2:1; 3:6, 8-9; 5:16, 18.

6. The Mosaic law. So see context.

7. H. Orton Wiley, *Christian Theology* (Kansas City: Beacon Hill Press of Kansas City, 1952), II, 508.

8. Charles Ewing Brown, *The Meaning of Salvation* (Anderson, Ind.: The Warner Press, 1944), p. 157.

9. Chafer, *op. cit.*, p. 288.

Chapter 4

1. Ralph M. Riggs, *The Spirit Himself* (Springfield, Mo.: The Gospel Publishing House, 1949). At the time the book was written, Mr. Riggs was an assistant general superintendent of the Assemblies of God with headquarters in Springfield, Mo.

2. Preface, page v.

3. E.g., by Charles Ewing Brown, *The Meaning of Sanctification* (Anderson, Ind.: The Warner Press, 1945), pp. 114-15.

4. *Op. cit.*, Chapters VII and VIII.

5. *Ibid.*, p. 47.

6. *The Person and Work of the Holy Spirit*, pp. 174, 176. Quoted by Riggs, *op. cit.*, pp. 47-48.

7. Chapter XIII.

8. *Ibid.*, p. 102.

9. *Ibid.*, p. 106.

10. *Ibid.*, p. 10.

11. *Ibid.*, p. 23.

12. *Ibid.*, p. 84.

13. *Ibid.*, pp. 84-85.

14. *Ibid.*, pp. 85-86.

15. *Ibid.*, p. 86.

16. A technical term meaning ecstatic utterance not ordinarily intelligible to those who speak or to those who hear.

17. Riggs, *op. cit.*, p. 89.

18. *Ibid.*, p. 97.

19. *Ibid.*, p. 164.

20. *Ibid.*, p. 86.

21. *Ibid.*, p. 89.

22. Adding Acts 4:30-31 and Acts 9:17 to the four described in Chapter 2.

CHAPTER 5

1. *Institutes of the Christian Religion*, II. xxi. 4, and xxi. 7.

2. *Op. cit.*, III, 269.

3. The careful Bible student will find the following references, among others, most convincing on this point: Isa. 45:22; 55:1; Ezek. 33:11; Matt. 11:28; Mark 16:15-16; John 1:12; 3:17; 12:47; Acts 2:21; 17:30; Rom. 1:16; 5:18; I Cor. 1:21; II Cor. 5:14-15, 19-20; Col. 1:28; I Tim. 2:1-6; Titus 2:11-12; Heb. 2:9; II Pet. 3:9; I John 2:1-2; Rev. 3:20; 22:17. Cf. R. A. Shank, *Elect in the Son* (Springfield, Mo., Westcott Publishers, 1970).

4. The "Five Points" include unconditional predestination,

limited atonement, total inability of man, irresistible grace, and final perseverance of the saints.

5. J. H. Strombeck, *Shall Never Perish* (Moline, Ill.: The Strombeck Agency, 900 23rd Ave., 1948). References here are to the sixth edition.

6. *Ibid.*, p. 1.

7. Cf. *ibid.*, p. 25.

8. *Ibid.*, p. 19.

9. *Ibid.*, p. 25.

10. *Ibid.*, p. 39.

11. John R. Rice, *Can a Saved Person Ever Be Lost?* p. 16.

12. August Van Ryn, *The Epistles of John* (New York: Loiseaux Brothers, 1948).

13. *Op. cit.*, p. 2.

14. *Ibid.*, p. 63.

15. In addition to the verses quoted, the following will be found relevant at this point: I Chron. 28:9; II Chron. 15:2; Ezek. 18:26; 33:18; Matt. 5:13; 10:22; 24:13; Mark 13:13; 16:16; Luke 9:62; John 15:1-2, 5-6; Rom. 8:13; 13:11; I Cor. 9:27; 10:1-12; II Cor. 6:1; I Tim. 1:19-20; 5:11-12, 15; II Tim. 2:10-11; Heb. 10:38; 12:15; Jas. 1:14-16; I Pet. 3:13; II Pet. 3:17; I John 2:24; 5:12; Jude 5-6; Rev. 2:4-5.

16. See Strombeck, *op cit.*, p. 136.

17. Douglas C. Hartley, "The Security of the Believer," *King's Business*, July, 1952, p. 9.